ANECDOTES OF BIG CATS
AND OTHER BEASTS

LECTOR HOUSE PUBLIC DOMAIN WORKS

This book is a result of an effort made by Lector House towards making a contribution to the preservation and repair of original classic literature. The original text is in the public domain in the United States of America, and possibly other countries depending upon their specific copyright laws.

In an attempt to preserve, improve and recreate the original content, certain conventional norms with regard to typographical mistakes, hyphenations, punctuations and/or other related subject matters, have been corrected upon our consideration. However, few such imperfections might not have been rectified as they were inherited and preserved from the original content to maintain the authenticity and construct, relevant to the work. The work might contain a few prior copyright references as well as page references which have been retained, wherever considered relevant to the part of the construct. We believe that this work holds historical, cultural and/or intellectual importance in the literary works community, therefore despite the oddities, we accounted the work for print as a part of our continuing effort towards preservation of literary work and our contribution towards the development of the society as a whole, driven by our beliefs.

We are grateful to our readers for putting their faith in us and accepting our imperfections with regard to preservation of the historical content. We shall strive hard to meet up to the expectations to improve further to provide an enriching reading experience.

Though, we conduct extensive research in ascertaining the status of copyright before redeveloping a version of the content, in rare cases, a classic work might be incorrectly marked as not-in-copyright. In such cases, if you are the copyright holder, then kindly contact us or write to us, and we shall get back to you with an immediate course of action.

HAPPY READING!

ANECDOTES OF BIG CATS AND OTHER BEASTS

DAVID ALEC WILSON

ISBN: 978-93-5420-248-3

Published: 1910

LECTOR HOUSE LLP
E-MAIL: lectorpublishing@gmail.com

Our good and true stories shall lighten our ills,
And songs to us comfort shall bring,
As long as the waters run down from the hills,
And trees bud afresh in the Spring.

ANECDOTES OF BIG CATS
AND OTHER BEASTS

BY

DAVID WILSON

THE BETTER THAT WE SEE THROUGH MEN,
THE GLADDER LOOK AT BEASTS AGAIN.

1910

CONTENTS

Page

CONTENTS   vii

ANECDOTES OF BIG CATS
AND OTHER BEASTS

I

THREE MEN TOGETHER

THE ideal hunter, like the ideal soldier or mountaineer, seaman or worker of any kind, "leaves nothing to chance"; yet in anticipating events he realises the limits of human foresight and remains continually wide-awake. Wellington has quoted Marshal Wrede's report of Napoleon's way of doing—to do from day to day what the circumstances require, but never have any general plan of campaign. That was how to rule circumstances by obeying them, as a seaman steering through the storm may be said to rule the waves. There are some occupations that allow more room for somnolence than others. Like the seaman afloat and the soldier in war, the man who is hunting big cats can ill afford to be caught napping. The consequences are apt to be sudden. It is a terrible thing to wake up from a nap with nothing to do but die.

Whether you are hunting thieves or tigers, you proceed by good guessing based on knowledge. There is no real difference between what is pompously called scientific reasoning and plain common-sense, as Huxley has elaborately shown. Thieves and tigers have their habits, like all living things, and need to eat to live. One of the commonest successful ways of coming to close quarters with "Mr Stripes" is to go to where he has been killing lately, and lie in ambush. If you persevere in doing that in the usual way, you are sure to meet the tiger in the long run; and perhaps, as happened to this writer in Burma, you may enjoy the pleasure of making his acquaintance with startling suddenness the very first time you try. So it is well to be ready for anything, lest you have a disagreeable experience, like three men in the Assam forests, whose adventure is worth telling, as a warning to beginners. The present writer heard it from Major Shaw (6th Gurkhas), in whom he has complete confidence. Of course it was in Assam that Major Shaw heard of it. For obvious reasons, no other names than his are given; and no superfluous details.

There is a public rest-house in the Assam woods, which was visited by a hungry tiger not many years ago. The caretaker (or "dirwan") was there at the time, but nobody else. The tiger took him away, and ate him.

Exactly how it was done remained unknown, as is usual in such cases. The men who are eaten by beasts of prey are generally like the crews of ships that never arrive, but remain for ever "missing." Not once in a thousand times can even the bones be found, and nothing was discovered in this instance, but nobody doubted what had happened. Nevertheless, a successor was soon installed in the dead man's place. The tiger called again; and once more the post became vacant, and a public servant was mysteriously "missing."

The caretaker of a rest-house, like the humble postman, is one of the few officials who appear to the non-official world to justify their existence. If it had been a forester or a policeman, a judge or a soldier, people would have shrugged their shoulders and said, "So much the worse for him." In the glad excitement of filling the vacancy, his colleagues would have forgotten him, and only his relatives, perhaps, if they had cause, lamented. But the caretakers of rest-houses are not luxuries but necessaries; and when either a second or a third man (Major Shaw could not recollect whether three caretakers or only two) had in this way disappeared into the hideous darkness that dimly veiled a hungry tiger, and there was a likelihood that travellers might be inconvenienced by the post remaining vacant, three men of public spirit arose and took their rifles, and went together to spend a night in the tiger-haunted bungalow, and give Mr Stripes a warm reception when he next came to call.

The oddest detail in the account of their preparations is that they fixed bayonets. The veranda was level with the floor of the building, apparently, and not far above the ground. It was reached from outside by a flight of steps, and ran along the front, with the doors of the rooms opening upon it. That was where the three men placed themselves, when they had finished dinner and arranged everything, fixed bayonets and all. They closed the doors, and supposed they were invisible, for the gleam of the lamplight was then restricted to the back and the side-windows. In front was only darkness visible. As they lay in wait there, the one in the middle would be where the caretaker was accustomed to lie, opposite the top of the stairs.

It must be remembered that the men perhaps expected to have to sit up several nights. They soon found what they had not expected, that it is very hard to keep awake, especially in a horizontal position, at the hour when you are usually asleep. Experienced hunters would have taken turns to lie in the middle wide-awake, and let the other men, on right and left, be at liberty to snooze. But these three men had been too excited to apprehend in advance the possibility of closing their eyes while waiting. They conversed in low whispers, and peered into the dark. Instead of coffee to keep them awake, as the night wore on, they drank whisky-and-soda.

The sound of a tropical forest is like London's noise, which never altogether stops, but what reached their ears was unexciting. The quadrupeds a-hunting were unseen, and flitted about as noiselessly as the clouds.

The three men slept. The man in the middle was suddenly jerked to his feet by the tight clasp of the tiger's jaws upon his forearm; and he staggered as it led him away, as if he had been a child. He was out of reach of his rifle before he was sufficiently awake to realise what was happening. It was afterwards conjectured that the tiger had been waiting below, and listening to their whispering, till the change of noises indicated sleep.

While the tiger, taking its man by the arm, was stepping downstairs, the man was thinking only, "I hope the bullet won't hit me." He never doubted that one of his companions was preparing to fire. But the other two men, awakened, and aware that the tiger had come, had taken refuge in a room, and supposed that he had done the same.

There was nothing very remarkable in the tiger pulling away the man in this way. That was probably how he had treated the caretakers. In their many millenniums of battle with mankind, and civilised mankind, not ill-armed negroes, such as make the lions bold, the tigers of the old world seem to have learned that the arms are the dangerous members of a man, like the poison fangs of a serpent, so that to seize them is to master him. There are many cases of a man being saved alive from a tiger by other men, when it was pulling him away by the arm; but I have never heard of any man so situated being able to deliver himself. In general, of course, it is easier to break a man's neck at once; but if you were a tiger, and your man were on a veranda, and had to be brought downstairs to be eaten comfortably, could you think of a better way than to pull him by the arm, and make him descend the stairs on his own legs? The tiger is a specialist in killing, and knows its business. It is not killing men that bothers the tiger, but catching them unawares.

So the tiger and the man together reached the bottom of the stairs without anything happening, and thence the tiger led towards the adjoining forest; but on the way the victim turned his face to the house as well as he could, and cried: "Are you fellows not going to help me?"

This was the first intimation of his fate to the other two. One of them came out and ran after the retreating figures of the tiger and the man disappearing down the pathway, going towards the woods, and overtook them in the nick of time. The shout had somehow affected the tiger too. He opened his jaws, and the mangled arm fell free; but a great paw was on the man's shoulder; and on the other shoulder another paw was now deliberately laid, and the tiger breathed in his face a deep, long exhalation—warm breath of a peculiar odour, that seemed to penetrate him.

Just then the pursuer arrived, and thrust his bayonet between the tiger's ribs, and pushed it in, and pulled the trigger. Then leaving the rifle there, feeling instinctively what Dr Johnson noticed in himself with surprise, when travelling in the Highlands, how willingly, in the dark, a man becomes "content to leave behind him everything but himself," he shouted "Follow me!" and ran back into the bungalow. The startled tiger had indeed let go its prey for the moment, but, seeing him run after the other man, it followed both; and, bounding up the stairs once more, it overtook at the top the man with the mangled arm, but only in time to give him a "smack on the back," which sent him flying through the doorway into the room where the others were. Then it died.

They washed the badly-bitten arm with whisky, having no medicaments of any kind. It would have been strange if they had had any, for men are so seldom hurt in tiger-shooting that nobody anticipates injury. They had nothing but whisky. So they poured it on, and "it nipped," at any-rate, which was, somehow, a comfort.

When the wounded man beheld himself in the looking-glass in the morning, he saw that his hair had suddenly grown grey in that one night. The third man, it is said, was delirious, with shame and remorse, because he had faltered. Meanwhile the tiger, growing stiff, lay dead on the veranda, just outside the door of the room, with a gaping wound in its side, like Thorwaldsen's lion at Lucerne.

When Major Shaw saw the injured man he had quite recovered. There was a scar on the arm, and a stiffness in two of the fingers, nothing else; but "for the rest of my life I could smell a tiger at fifty yards," said he. "I'll never forget the smell that went through me as he breathed upon me—never, as long as I live."

II

THE WONDERFUL ESCAPE OF "TIGER-HILL"

I AM sorry to say it is more than twenty years since I began to listen to stories of tigers and leopards in Burma; and even more since I first made acquaintance with the beasts myself. I do not expect to see any more now, except in a Zoo. So perhaps it is time to note what has been learned, to re-tell the best of what I have heard, and in short do for others what others in days gone by have done for me. I have always considered that the man who keeps a good story fresh is the greatest of public benefactors.

What made me think of this in connection with cats was the recent discovery of the truth of a story, which I have heard many times without believing it. It was first told to me in 1891 by Burmans in the locality where it happened. Then, and as often afterwards as it was told, I questioned the speaker about how he knew, and never was quite satisfied. Even the version of it in Colonel Pollok's *Wild Sports of Burma and Assam* (p. 65 of the 1900 edition), read like hearsay and seemed unconvincing. At last, in 1908, Colonel Dobbs told it to me in Coonoor, and when he was questioned he was able to delight me with the news that he had *seen* the thing. So here it is.

The time was 1859. The scene was the forest-covered hilly ground about seventy miles north of Maulmain, in what is now Bilin township of Thaton district, Burma, between the Sittang and Salween rivers. A detachment of the 32nd Madras Native Infantry, under Captain Manley, was marching on business there, going in single file along a footpath, preceded by the civil officer with them, a Mr Charles Hill.

Hill was a big man, "over six feet and of great strength," and strode ahead with a big stick in his hand, while two orderlies or servants followed at a careless distance behind him, with his weapons. This Chinese way of making war or hunting is almost a custom in Burma among Europeans; and a very natural custom too, in a hot, moist climate.

Suddenly Hill came upon a tiger lying full length on the footpath, apparently asleep. He looked round and called for his gun. It was for the moment out of reach.

Perhaps it may be worth while to try to make the ordinary stay-at-home Englishman, who does not know how lucky he is to be able to stay at home, and knows a great deal less than he supposes, realise how and why the sensations of Mr Hill were different from what his own would have been. The first point is that Hill knew what a Londoner would never suspect, that there was no particular cause to be afraid. If afraid, he had only to go back a few yards, and shout, and bang the trees with his stick. The monstrous cat would take the hint and silently slip away. Not even a tiger in the prime of life would *seek* a fight. He feels, what politicians are only beginning to realise in another sphere, that fighting is bad business.

We must remember that the tiger has no medicaments, no surgical help, no hospitals, no friends, no companions. When he crawls away to lick his wounds, he is as solitary in a hostile world as a poor man "out of a job," on a wet wintry night on the Thames Embankment, and suffers and dies unaided and alone. This is not conducive to courage. So even a tiger that has taken to eating men does not openly attack humanity, but lies in wait for it, to take it by surprise without fighting, seeking nothing but to get his dinner in the easiest way. Our common criminals, and many wholesale thieves of superficial respectability, are more dangerous than tigers because of their extra cunning, but not different in spirit. What difference there is, is in favour of the tiger. He is never malevolent or cruel. Like Jonathan Wild, he never hurts anybody, except to benefit himself.

The Englishman at home will perhaps now be ready to understand the next point that will surprise him, that the retiring habits of the tiger make him a rare sight, even in countries where he is at home. I have known many people who had often suffered from the depredations of tigers, but had never seen one, just as a man's house may be burgled more than once without his seeing any of the burglars. The tiger is like a burglar, who comes and goes in the dark.

It is true that a globe-trotter visiting Rangoon to-day (1909) may buy on the Pagoda steps a picture of a tiger upon the Pagoda, and be truly told that it was seen there. Some years ago a tiger did go up the gentle slope of the spire; and once arrived there, he stood bewildered, as if paralysed; conspicuous, like a weather-cock upon a steeple, looking helplessly down upon a large port like Plymouth, a big animated and terrified target, while the soldiers shot at him till they killed him. But though Englishmen, who knew there were tigers always near, might think this natural, and only wonder that it did not happen oftener, and wish it would, yet to the people of the country, who knew the habits of tigers, it seemed portentous. Long afterwards old men might be seen on the Pagoda platform shaking their heads knowingly, and if you listened and understood them, you could hear them discussing what the miracle meant. It was certainly very odd. The poor animal must somehow have lost his reckoning. To use an old-fashioned phrase, he was never intended for a town life, and assuredly he never intended to try it. The Pagoda stands on the skirts of the town, on the last bluff of the Pegu hills, and he was probably going up it before he knew he had left the woods.

An incident that took place near the scene of Mr Hill's adventure may be mentioned to illustrate the normal ways of the tiger. Three officers united to assist the villagers there against a tiger that was thinning their herds. Each of them had killed big cats before; and one was locally famous as a hunter. His house was full of trophies, including scores of tiger skins, of which he was as proud as ever Red Indian was of scalps. About a hundred villagers who knew the ground well co-operated zealously. No mistakes were made, and everybody did his best for several days; and yet not one of the large party ever even saw the beast they were seeking. He had not gone away. He was lying low; and he resumed his cattle killing as soon as they stopped hunting. The widest "beat" in woods like these is like a net flung at random into the sea. A hunter is lucky if he averages a single glimpse of such game for half-a-dozen days or nights out of bed. Experienced hunters seldom go out there after tiger except to spend a night in a tree over a "kill," which is generally a bullock killed and left half eaten, to which the tiger may return.

So it is easy to understand why Hill was unwilling to lose sight of this fellow, especially if Colonel Pollok is rightly informed that it was a man-eater; for in that part of Burma the occasional man-eater is not only a public affliction, he is also more often than not old and decrepit. I saw one in the Sittang valley, which had killed three men in one week, and yet was a meagre creature, with shrunken shanks and bald, bare hide, which made him look mangy, and with only a single whole tooth in his jaws, and two broken ones. So if Hill had heard the rumour which Colonel Pollok believed and took this for a man-eater, he might reasonably suppose he could take liberties. The canny Dutch themselves have a proverb, that the hares can pull the lion's beard when the lion has grown old.

It is a witty exaggeration, of course, as proverbs often are. In reality, neither hares nor horses nor deer of any kind would risk going near a lion or a tiger, however old. They shrink in horror from the like of a tiger. I have felt a brave horse shudder at one although he was dead, for even in death he seemed terrible. But his carcass does not cumber long the ground. White ants have a horror of nothing, and maggots and microbes, safe in their insignificance, are equally impartial. Vultures, too, may serve the tiger for undertakers, as they serve the Parsis, or the wild dogs may anticipate them. Sometimes it has been credibly reported that the dogs begin the tiger's funeral before he is dead, so that if only the Dutch had said "dogs" instead of "hares" their proverb would have been *not* wit but natural history.

Even if Hill had never heard about this tiger being a stiff old man-eater, he might have suspected it was one, because it was there, upon the footpath, as if it had fallen asleep while watching for some benighted traveller who might be caught unawares. The few seconds Hill stood waiting for a gun would seem as many minutes, or more. In short, it is easy to imagine how, as he watched the big beast, perhaps stretching itself and yawning, seeming likely to step aside soon, before a gun arrived, into a wood wherein a few steps would make it safe from pursuit, the big strong man lost patience, and lifting his stick with both hands he hit the tiger on the head between the eyes.

This completed the wakening process. Hill said he only saw it disappear among the bushes at the side of the path. Meanwhile Lieutenant Dobbs (he was *young* Dobbs then and on duty under Captain Manley) happened to be nearest to the front after Hill, and he and some sepoys hurried forward. In jungle fighting you run to the shouting, just as in ordinary war the rule used to be to march towards the sound of the cannon. So Dobbs, running forward in this way, was in time to see what followed. It was all over in a few seconds, and the reproaches of the troops in some histories of the event are without foundation. The tiger leapt out of the bush towards Hill's back, and with a paw on each of his shoulders was seen to be biting at the back of his neck, as if trying to get a grip. Then Hill, who had been flung forward into a stooping posture, but kept his foothold, straightened himself with a jerk, whirled round and thrust out his arms in front of him, with open palms, as if pushing. "That, at least, is what it seemed like to me," said the accurate veteran, Colonel Dobbs, and that was how Hill described it. Then the tiger fell backwards, rolled on his back, regained his balance with a soft, silent celerity, and disappeared again among the bushes "almost like lightning," and was seen no more.

Hill came staggering towards Dobbs, and fell on his face in a dead faint. He was bleeding freely from the neck, but the bleeding was soon stopped. "Only the upper fangs penetrated the neck," writes Colonel Pollok. What Dobbs was sure of was only that in a short time Hill was going about as usual, "though he complained of stiff neck for about two years afterwards."

In 1891 the Burmans thereabouts were still speaking of him as "Kya-ma-na-ing," meaning "The man that the tiger did not beat." He was honourably known to his countrymen in Burma for the rest of his life as "Tiger-Hill"; and the many and various versions of his adventure might furnish texts for a book on mythology as long as Fraser's three big volumes on the *Golden Bough*. But as nearly all the reflections hitherto made upon it are refuted by this mere statement of the details, the present writer will take warning from the mistakes of his predecessors and leave readers, now in possession of the truth, to evolve their own reflections.

III

SHERLOCK HOLMES IN A WOOD

ON 20th April 1895, being engaged in Forest Settlement work among the low hills abutting on the south the mountain barrier between Burma and Assam, I was aroused, as I sat reading in a tent in the afternoon, by a signal. It meant that my colleague, Mr Bruce, the Deputy Conservator of Forests, who had gone out to shoot pigeons for dinner, either was or expected soon to be in contact with tiger, and wished me to join him—which I did, at a run. He was near the camp. The tigers thereabouts are more plentiful than elsewhere in Burma. We had seen and heard abundant evidence of their proximity for weeks past, and were both anxious for a closer acquaintance.

A fat and full-grown deer was lying dead upon the stones in a stream-bed. The first guess was that a tiger, having killed, was about to eat it, but withdrew for a moment out of sight at the sound of the pigeon-shooting. On this hypothesis we diligently searched in all likely directions, and made sure there was no tiger near. Then we gathered round the deer. A faint, faint smell, perceptible as we closed upon it, showed that the venison was tending to that disintegration which awaits all flesh when life departs, and answered those who were beginning to doubt if it was dead, because it lay as if it might have been asleep, and there was no sign to show how it had died.

"Twelve to twenty-four hours dead, and not killed by any tiger," was the first unanimous conclusion, after minute inspection and confabulation; and "still fresh enough to be eaten" was the next decision, all but equally unanimous.

This satisfied most of the men; but Bruce stood silent, while they knelt round it and began to ply their knives. I stayed to await developments. Casting perplexed looks up and down the stream, Bruce ejaculated, more than once, "I would give anything to know how that beast died." "It's too soft to roast, but will make splendid curry," said the cook, inspecting a joint cut from the carcass.

When the men had cut off about three times as much as would suffice to "abate their desire of food," they began obligingly to discuss what was puzzling Bruce, and in a short time, so lively are the Burmese wits, every man seemed to be as interested as himself in the apparently insoluble problem. A mystery attracts men, as a light does the moths; or, as Cicero explains it in his *Offices* (i.4)—"The peculiarity of man is to seek and follow after truth. So, as soon as we are relaxed from our necessary cares and concerns, what we covet is to see, to hear, and to learn something; and the knowledge of things obscure or wonderful quickly appears to us to be indispensable for our comfort and happiness."

Wild dogs were as likely as a tiger to have killed that deer; but equally certain not to leave the dead uneaten. The wild dogs and the tigers alike are real professional hunters, who kill in order to be able to eat and live. They are not sportsmen, who kill for amusement, that is to say, for want of occupation. Besides, there were no marks discoverable of either a tiger or dogs.

The partition of the venison served the purpose of a post-mortem. When it was seen that the neck was broken, we looked at the steep ground on the northern bank and saw how the deer could have tumbled down; and "killed by a fall" was the first step to a final verdict.

But why did it fall? It was useless to suggest, as one did, "committed suicide in a temporary state of insanity." He was gravely assured on every hand that the deer, however worried, do not commit suicide.

It would be long to tell the other guesses. Nobody could find a scratch on the carcass. That alone disposed of many theories.

Bruce had for some time spoken only in interjections. His mind was working. Suddenly he cried, with the abrupt inspiration of a seer, "I have it! I have it! I see what it was. This stag and another fought for a hind on that high bank, and this was the one pushed over."

We agreed. Some of us would have agreed to anything, being tired of the subject. But we really were convinced; and when Bruce had finished describing the probable (what a blessed word probable is, to be sure!—the probable) antlers of the victor, contrasting them with the poor young brow of the dead, there were some among us who would in a little time have been capable of describing in a witness-box the aforesaid victorious antlers as things seen and handled. It was a doubter who said, "If you're right the tracks of the fighters must be visible yet. It cannot have been before last night. The ground seems soft up there, and there has been no rain."

As soon as the words were spoken, as if by one consent, the men tore up the steep, Bruce shouting something that sounded like, "Right you are, for once!" On hands and knees went some; and they distributed themselves, to miss nothing, panting, puffing, all climbing as if a golden fleece awaited their joint efforts, and earnestly scanning the ground as they went. They did not compete though they vied with each other, each helping his neighbour, in a genial way; and, joyfully working together, they unconsciously illustrated the solidarity of humanity in real life.

Soon they were rejoicing and jubilating as loudly as if a heap of golden fleeces had been found, for they saw the tracks they went to seek. The duel of the stags, as it must have happened in the cool starlight of the preceding night, could be traced and rehearsed from the hieroglyphics on the ground by the sharpened wits of the village specialists, with more confidence than the incidents of a battle can be deciphered by a historian. Here it was, in a narrow glade, that they charged and grappled; there and there they struggled and pushed to and fro till one went backwards, and there at last, as you could see, one backed over the steep and stumbled suddenly into death, to lie on the stones below, until we came and, anticipating other carrion-eaters, cut him up for dinner.

"And now, let's track the victor!"

Heigh-ho! It was to face a tiger I laid down my book, and not to follow an amorous deer; but the tracks led into the stream again. "The victor went for a drink," we said to each other, like children rejoicing to find that they can draw an inference for themselves, or rather like men who have learned, as all men do at last, how liable they are to be mistaken, and are slow to feel sure of anything till they find that others agree.

Among the stones the tracks were lost. Then I recalled how Robert the Bruce of Bannockburn had baffled the bloodhounds following him once, in his days of difficulty, by walking along a stream; and I suggested that the deer might in the same way baffle a modern Bruce. But men are more knowing than bloodhounds.

"The stag is not a water-buffalo. He'll quench his thirst and leave the stream. Won't he?"

"He must have done so, for he isn't here."

"The banks aren't rocks. We'll see where he left as well as where he came, won't we?"

"Assuredly you shall, if you look long enough. I'll stay ten minutes."

"I'll stay till dark."

It was not needed. The men started to seek the trail with enthusiasm; and in a few minutes there was a joyful shout and soon we were following the vanished stag, as confidently as if he were bodily in front of us, along one of the deer-paths that were a feature of these primeval woods. Our Burmans were admirable. Plain villagers, but all-round men, observant, they could notice swiftly and surely the slightest marks on the surface of the path which were signs of recent tracks. They had a rare reward. Few modern events have caused to sated Europeans the sensations they experienced when, instead of the expected jumble of many prints, to show where our wanderer rejoined his fellows, or at least his partner, they came upon the clean-picked bones and antlers of the stag at the side of the path, and a few fresh tiger-tracks that showed how he in turn had died....

"I like this, I like to get to the bottom of things. I'm glad we came," cried Bruce. "This is the kind of thing that makes you realise what life in the forests truly is...."

"Beasts for beasts," said his companion, "if one has to deal with beasts, the four-legged varieties here are simple and almost harmless compared to the rascals on two legs...."

Bruce was urgent upon me to write out this authentic idyll of the woods which he had elucidated. I had to promise; but I did it vaguely—"when I have time," "when I retire," "when the spirit moves me"—so that time was not of the essence of the contract. It never occurred to me that there was any need to hurry on his account, for he was the younger man; but now I wish I had kept my promise sooner.

For Bruce is dead.

<h1 style="text-align:center">IV</h1>

<h1 style="text-align:center">WHERE TIGERS FLOURISH</h1>

1. TIGERS IN THE AIR

IN 1895, while doing Forest Settlement work in the Upper Chindwin district of Upper Burma, I lived in an atmosphere of tigers. Hardly a day passed without seeing or hearing some sign of them. It was a great disappointment, both to my companion and colleague, Mr Bruce, Deputy Conservator of Forests, and to myself to finish our long journeyings without a single encounter. We spared no pains to compass one; but we were going fast, with a troop of elephants for baggage, and were being met at many points by crowds of men on business; so that it was not a surprise, although it was a disappointment, to miss seeing "our friend the enemy" at home. The tiger, as we were well aware, might say with Tommy Atkins that he is fighting for meat and not for glory; and when, in seeking dinner, he caught sight of an enemy that seemed dangerous, he was bound to behave like Brer Rabbit, to lie low and say nothing. The jungle was continuous, and in parts so thick that he might at times have been lying within spitting distance and remained unseen and unsuspected.

No doubt the tigers saw us many a time, though we saw none of them. The villagers, in order to feel safe, went about in twos and threes or in larger parties, like London policemen in the slums. Whenever two parties met, they discussed the latest news of tigers. Among a crowd of items, I well recollect that both Mr Dickinson, the Conservator, and Mr Bruce had much to tell me about the fine performances of C. W. Allan of their department that year there, and of his experiences in 1894.

As "half a word fixed, upon or near the spot, is worth a cart-load of recollection," according to authority, I have persuaded Mr Allan, now Deputy Conservator at Henzada, to let me publish a few extracts from his *Shikar-Book*, a contemporary record. It may be as well to mention that, knowing him well, I believe what he wrote as firmly as if I had seen it all myself, and that it tallies completely with what was told me in 1895.

2. TIGERS VICTORIOUS

[Extract from the "Shikar-Book" of C. W. Allan]

"DURING the month of March, 1894, I had to go out into the Kubo Valley, in the Kindat Forest Division, Upper Chindwin, to do the demarcation of the Khanpat Reserve. On the 16th I arrived at the village of Thinzin and halted there the 17th to collect coolies to do the work, which I found to be no easy matter. On inquiring the reason, I was told that there was a man-eater tiger in that part of the forest, and that it had killed three men within the last six weeks, and that people were afraid to go anywhere near the forest. This was very unpleasant news. However, the work had to be done and men must be found, so I ordered the Thugyi (village headman) to hurry up and get them, and told him that there was nothing to be afraid of as I had five guns with me and could look after the men.

"On questioning the Thugyi about the man-eater, he informed me that the first man killed was a mahout (elephant driver) employed by the Bombay Burma Trading Corporation. This man was carried off in the Pyoungbok stream. He and another man had gone out to look for their elephant, which had been fettered and turned out to graze. And it was whilst following up the drag of the chain that the tiger sprang on to the mahout who was leading, and was carrying a gun on his shoulder, and carried him off. The man who was following the mahout was carrying a dah (big knife) in his hand, and was just behind the mahout. He was so taken aback that he could do nothing to save his companion, so ran away and informed some other men who were encamped close by. But they were too frightened to go and look for the mahout. And it would not have been much good their going, for by the time they got to the place the tiger would have finished his meal and moved off.

"The second man carried off was also a mahout in the service of the B. B. T. C. He was also carried off much in the same manner from the Nansawin stream, and within ten days of the date the first man was killed. This mahout was out with a party of some six men hunting for fish in the stream, when the tiger sprang on to him from the bank and carried him off before the other men could do anything. They too did not attempt to save their comrade, but made tracks out of that stream as fast as their legs could carry them.

"The third man killed was a Burmese policeman. A party of six constables were out on patrol, and had camped for the night under a large teak tree between the Pyoungbok and Nansawin streams. About four o'clock in the morning one of the men had got up and lit a fire, and put on a pot of rice to boil for their breakfast, and had lain down again beside the other men, intending to have another forty winks. He had barely laid himself down when a tiger sneaked up behind the tree they were sleeping under and seized the end man by the waist and carried him off. The poor man shouted for all he was worth, 'Shoot, shoot, the tiger is carrying me off.' This roused the others and they picked up their guns and tried to shoot, but the powder or caps being damp, the charges would not go off. They, however, put on fresh caps and eventually got the guns to shoot. After this they fired several shots and shouted, but the man's cries had stopped, so they judged that he must have been killed.

"The constables waited at their camp till daylight, and then went off to the camp of some Burmese elephant drivers, which was about three miles off, and made them collect their elephants, some seventeen in number, and then returned and looked for their comrade. They found the remains within a couple of hundred yards of their night's camp. The tiger had finished its meal and had gone off. The Thugyi informed me that although several shots had been fired in the direction the tiger had gone it was not frightened, and sat there and finished its meal.

"Hearing all this, I did not wonder at the men not wanting to go into the forest. However, the work had to be done and go I must. Though I must admit I did not quite appreciate the job."

3. WORKING ALONGSIDE

"ON the morning of the 18th March some twenty men turned up, and the Thugyi informed me that the others would follow. So I made a move and got as far as the Khanpat stream, where I halted for a bit and had breakfast and then moved on again. It was my intention to make the Pyoungbok camp that day, as I was told it had a fence round it, made by the patrols to keep out the tiger. But the coolies would not move fast enough, so I camped on the Nanpalon stream.

"After seeing the camp pitched and everything in place, I told my clerk to make all the men stay together, and not to let any men go about the forest in ones and twos, for fear of the tiger. I also told him to have a big fire burning and to keep a watch of five men at the fire and to relieve them every two hours, and to call me in case of an alarm.

"I turned into bed at about nine o'clock, and had not been in bed ten minutes when the clerk came and called me, saying the tiger had come. I jumped out of bed, and taking my rifle ran out. The men at the fire told me that a pony tied near them began to get very restless, and kept looking towards the stream, so they got up and looked, and saw the tiger not twenty paces off, ready to rush at them. I asked where it had gone to on being found out. They replied that it had gone down into the stream.

"Whilst I was talking to the men, one man, who was looking in the direction of the stream, said, 'Look, sir, there it is, going up the bank,' and sure enough there it was, about seventy yards off, going across the bed of the stream. I had a shot and it sprang up the bank, and just as it was disappearing I fired a second shot. All the men said I had hit it, and Maung Kyaw Nya, my forester, was for going and looking for blood, but I thought this too dangerous and would not let him go. The next morning we got up early and went and had a look at the place where the tiger had been standing when I fired at it. I found where both the bullets had struck the ground. They were both clean misses, and had struck below the tiger and between its legs."

(*N.B.*—Mr Allan was and is one of the best hunters in Burma; but, in firing in the dark, one cannot see one's sights, and so the best of shots makes misses.—D. W.)

"For the next three days nothing happened and the coolies seemed to have got over their fright and were working well.

"On the 23rd I moved camp to a place on the Nansawin stream. The forest there was very dense and I did not at all like the idea of camping there, but as that was the only place where there was water, I had a place cleared and pitched my tent, and then went out to inspect the work. I gave orders to Maung Kyaw Nya to go ahead and pick out the way the line of demarcation should go in, and also to see how far the Thonhmwason" (that is, Three-Waters-Meeting, a camping-place where three streams met) "was from my camp of that day.

"At 3 p.m. a man came to me from the camp and said that Mg. Kyaw Nya had returned, as he had been chased by a tiger. On my return to camp in the evening I sent for Kyaw Nya and questioned him as to why he had not carried out my order. He replied that he and two other men were going along the foot of the hill following the boundary, when they came on to a half-eaten sambur (big deer). They were going to take the flesh and bring it to camp for their dinner, when they heard a rustling in the leaves, and on looking round saw a tiger coming to see what they wanted with its dinner. The men, seeing the tiger coming, dropped the sambur and went for all they were worth, till they got out into the bed of the stream, and then came down it to my camp.

"I thought the men were afraid to go out by themselves to locate the boundary, and had invented the yarn about the tiger. Mg. Kyaw Nya said, 'If you do not believe me, sir, I will show you the place.'

"On the morning of the 25th I went out with Mg. Kyaw Nya and three or four men, and they took me to the place where the tiger's kill had been, and sure enough there had been a kill there, but it had been finished off during the night and there was nothing but the skull and feet left. On my return to camp I had tea, and was thinking of tying out a goat and sitting up for the tiger, but I did not like the idea of having to get off the machan (platform made in a tree) and come back to the tent in the dark, so I gave it up."

(Another objection, fatal to this plan, was that the men would have been afraid to stay in the camp at night by themselves.—D. W.)

"About 4 p.m. the men were returning from work, when I heard a great shouting not far from camp, so went out in the direction and met them returning. The forester in charge informed me that a tiger had charged out at the line of men and had tried to take one from the centre, and that the man had thrown his dah (big knife) at the beast, on which it bolted back into the grass."

4. AT VERY CLOSE QUARTERS

"ON seeing that the tiger was round our camp I took extra precautions and made all the men stop in one place just behind my tent; and gave orders to my Indian servants to have their dinner early, and to sleep with the Burmese coolies. My cook, an Indian, would not stop near the Burmans, though told to do so several times. He had his kitchen fire just in front of my tent. However, I told him he must sleep with the other men. The other Indians also told him not to be a fool and stay away by himself. To them he replied that he was not afraid, and that if it was his fate the tiger would have him. He said, 'If it takes me, it will be a case of one crunch and all will be over,' and this is just what happened.

"I was having dinner early, before it got quite dark, so as to get the men together. The cook had given me my soup and had cleared the plate and put a roast fowl before me, and had gone back to the fire and was standing with a knife in his hand watching the pudding on the fire.

"I was just carving the chicken, when I heard the cook give a frightened cry, and on looking up I saw the tiger spring on to the cook. In jumping up I upset the table and the lamp on it, also a glass of beer that had just been poured out for me, and ran out shouting at the tiger, and threw my table knife at it. My dogs, two terriers and a spaniel, were sitting by my table, and jumped up and ran after the tiger with me and attacked it. One terrier and the spaniel were killed on the spot, and the other dog got away. In spite of this the tiger went off with the cook. I thought the tiger had got the cook by the back, but the sweeper who was standing close by with my goats" (that is to say, had been there when the tiger came), "said it had got him by the head, and so it turned out to be the case.

"On hearing me shout, the sweeper ran into the tent and got my rifle and cartridges and handed them to me. I put in a cartridge and fired in the direction the tiger had gone, and this had the effect of making him drop the cook, but we did not know it at the time as no one would venture into the forest to look for him. This of course upset everyone in camp, and all huddled round my tent as close as they could and shouted and beat tins all night. No one would even go to replenish the fire unless I went with them, though it was not three yards from my tent. All that night the tiger kept moving round the tent and I kept it off by firing shots whenever we heard it walking in the leaves and saw its eyes shining like live coals in the dark."

Here it may be noted that the eyes of a tiger, shining through the blackness of the utter dark, are a phenomenon hard to forget, if once you see them. In this instance, whatever strange light shone in them may have been intensified by the glare of the camp-fire reflected in those glistening optics. But no such addition was possible in another case credibly reported to me and of more recent date in the extreme north of Burma. A tiger ventured into the sepoy lines one night, and entering the open door of a hut, it killed and carried away a man asleep in bed. His comrades chased and mobbed the beast, which dropped the corpse and escaped. The sepoys, taking counsel together, put out the lights and hushed all noises, as if everyone was asleep; and in fact they were back in their huts, and the door of the dead man's dwelling stood open as before. Only, in ambush, below or beside the bed, in a dark corner, a brave man was waiting, rifle ready; and the tiger did come back to that identical door that night, and was shot, exactly as the sepoys had hoped. What lingers in the memory best, of all the details of that adventure, is that the man who lay in wait told a magistrate, who told me, that when the tiger came, all he saw was "the eyes in the doorway, shining into the room like two coloured lamps, filling the room with tinted light." So he felt that hiding was impossible and "banged away."

One other remark may be intercalated, to let readers realise what is what. Even to men of experience in tiger attacks, the swift suddenness of events is a continual surprise. The tiger practises "surprise tactics," and his attack often is, and always is when he can manage it, like a railway collision—it takes long to tell, but only a few seconds to happen.

Let us now return to Mr Allan's journal.

"Early next morning, as soon as it was light enough to see, I started to look for the body of the cook, and found it not ten paces from where he had been cooking. The jungle, as I said before, was very thick, so we could not see it at night."

(The tiger must have dropped the corpse when Mr Allan fired. He had therefore lost his supper. Probably enough that was why he continued prowling round.—D. W.)

"The tiger had caught the cook by the head as the sweeper had said, for one fang had gone into his right eye and had knocked it out, another had gone into his throat just below the chin, and two had gone into the skull and neck at the back. So it must have taken the whole head into its mouth, for it was a pulp with the brains coming out.

"We dug a shallow grave for the poor old cook and buried him, and then left that forest as fast as the men could lay legs to the ground, for nothing would induce them to stop another hour.... They yelled and shouted till they got right clear of the forest.

"In leaving the forest no one wanted to be the last in the line for fear of being taken from the back, so I brought up the rear."

It only remains to be added that in 1895, though the tigers "remained as usual," Mr Allan finished the demarcation work so tragically interrupted, and even took his wife to see the grave of the cook.

5. THE CHARGE OF THE TIGRESS

COMING to 1909, there is an episode in his *Shikar-Book* about a tigress, which for various reasons may be transcribed:—

"... 14th April.—I started up to inspect the Banbwebin fire line ... accompanied by my wife ... an Indian and two Burmans.... After we had gone about five miles up the ... path, ... we heard bamboos being broken. The Burmans said there must be a herd of wild elephants feeding on the flowered bamboos. I thought they might possibly be bison or a rhinoceros, so walked on to see what they really were. The Indian was walking ahead of me, and I was following, looking down the side of the hill from which the sound of the bamboos being broken came, when Barhan, the Indian peon, stopped and said 'Bag' (tiger). I looked up and saw the tiger crossing the path about sixty paces ahead of me, so ... had a quick shot at it. On which it turned round and came down the hill straight at me.... My wife, who was just behind me, on seeing it come down the hill, called out, 'It is coming.' ... It came on, and when less than thirty paces from me I fired the second barrel and knocked it over. After receiving the shot it fell and lay on the ground, trying to drag itself towards us.... It put its head up and snarled and showed its teeth.... The Burmans, who were very excited, kept on saying, 'Give it another shot quick, or it will get up and do for us.' So after a bit I put in another cartridge and walked up a few paces and gave it a bullet in the chest and finished it off.

"After giving it a shot in the chest I walked round and got above it, and then approached cautiously with my gun at the ready to give it another shot if necessary; but after throwing a clod or two of earth at it, and finding that it did not move, I walked up and pulled its tail, and when I found that it was dead I called out to my wife, who was close by all the time, and she came up.

"We found it to be a tigress ... measuring eight feet and five inches as she lay.... The first shot had missed and the second ... caught her at the point of the shoulder. On looking at my gun, I found that the 200 yards leaf sight had got pushed up, and that made me shoot high. I was carrying the gun in my right hand, but holding it across my back, and in pulling it forward in a hurry, the leaf sight had got pushed up, and I did not notice it in the excitement of the moment....

"Maung Nita, one of the Burmans who was with me, said, 'Sir, if you had not finished her with the second shot we would all have been lying kicking on the ground.'

"As three men were not able to lift her, my wife rode back to our camp and called other eight men, and they slung her on poles and carried her into camp.

"On dissecting the tigress, I found that she had nothing in her stomach and appeared to have had no food for some time. She was evidently out shikaring (hunting), and was after the animals that I heard breaking bamboos." ...

In a private letter to me at the time, Mr Allan wrote:—

"... Had I missed the second shot she would have had us.... She was very angry. She was hungry and meant business. On opening her we found that she ... had evidently not had a meal for some days." ... This illustrates a truth which is often forgotten by us. The big beasts live from hand to mouth, like improvident working men. A dog may bury a bone, a tiger return to a kill, and a leopard has been known to put half a corpse or an unfinished bit of venison up a tree for security. But beyond the next meal they never look. It is only the insects of the universe, like ants and bees, or such animals as squirrels, that practise thrift. Hence arose the Jewish proverb about considering the ways of the ant in order to be wise. There is no such lesson to be learned from the cat.

One can be sorry for the tigress all the same. Think of her empty stomach, and perhaps hungry cubs in her lair; and then this big, strong Englishman, with his diabolical machinery in his hand, molesting her as she was stalking the wild cattle. "She meant business," said he. Of course she did. Did anyone think she was hunting for amusement?

No matter now! Her body lies inert enough, a subject for their inquisitive knives to her indifferent.

Put yourself in the skin of that tigress, if you can. Think what a gunshot means to a wild beast, and consider how, when fired at, she "faced the music" in the real sense of that phrase, and went "straight at the guns," as gallantly as the Light Brigade at Balaklava. As even the enemy notes—"After receiving the shot, _it fell and lay on the ground, trying to drag itself towards us.... It put its head up and snarled and showed its teeth._" ... Was she not like the glorious Englishman, who, when his legs were cut away, still fought upon his stumps? Did any hero of Homer's ever surpass that sorely-stricken tigress? Could any living creature have done more? And yet there are men to be found who call the big cats cowards! I never heard Mr Allan do that, nor any other man of sense who knew them well at first hand.

No wonder tigers flourished in the days of old. It is the invention of gunpowder, and then of breechloaders, that has handicapped them hopelessly. The long guerilla war between them and us has lasted for scores of millenniums; but the end is now in sight. Let us not libel the brave that are doomed to disappear. Let us not rail at the conquered. If they were fierce and strong, they were not cruel. As Nature made them, so they filled their function. They came, and chased, and conquered, impelled by hunger: and now that their hour has come they are going away. The day is at hand when the big wild cats shall all be as completely extinct as the vanished giants that wallowed in the primeval slime.

V

THE GIRL AND THE TIGRESS

THIS is a story that has been often told; and I confess I did not believe it when I heard it in 1895, in the district where it happened. Long afterwards, in 1908, Mr G. Tilly, who had been the District Superintendent of Police on the spot at the time, told me he held a local inquiry, and was so completely satisfied of the truth of it that he recommended the payment of a reward of R100 to the girl, and the Deputy Commissioner and the Commissioner agreed with him, and the Chief Commissioner of Burma sanctioned the reward, which was paid. In the absence of any motive for rash credulity on the part of these officers, this might seem enough; but I happened to be acquainted with Mr Grant Brown, who is now the Deputy Commissioner of that district, called the Upper Chindwin, and wrote to him about it. He replied on 21/2/09: "... I remembered the incident quite well as told in the *Rangoon Gazette*, and should have included it in my article on Burmese women if I had been able to remember more of the details; but I had no idea that it took place in this district. Curiously enough, the very first person I asked was the headman of the village where the thing happened. He could give me no details beyond those you mention.... The heroine is dead, and as I thought I was sure to find an account of what happened in the record-room I did not make further inquiries. A search has been made, however, without result...."

The "article" mentioned is Mr Grant Brown's article in *The Women of all Nations*, by Messrs Joyce & Thomas, published by the Messrs Cassell lately.

Failing to find the record of the original inquiry held by Mr Tilly, which had perished, as a thing no longer needed, in a periodical destruction of papers, Mr Grant Brown had a new inquiry held, and the vernacular record of it is now before me. I sent a set of interrogatories, which have been answered by Ma Shway U, an eye-witness, and the head man of the village and another man, who were soon on the scene, measured the tigress and did everything else that needed to be done. None of these persons has any motive for misstatement, and the chance of mistake is infinitesimal. That time has not altered their stories I can myself testify, for what they say tallies with what I was told in 1895.

Readers can now see how my doubts have been removed, and must be impatient to know what it was that I was so slow to believe. As Mr Tilly tells me the newspapers merely gave more or less abbreviated versions of his report, I have not referred to them.

The scene was Seiktha village on the Chindwin, an Upper Burman tributary of the Irrawaddy, in one of the districts that form the southern fringe of the mountains between Burma and Assam. One day in 1894 three nut-brown girls set out from Seiktha to cut firewood in the forest, making for a likely place they knew, a little south-east of their village. They carried one or two heavy knives or choppers, like butchers' cleavers, such as are common in Burman houses.

Now if there had only been a man with them, or even a big boy, he would certainly there and then, in going and coming, have walked in front, bearing a spear or dah, a big curved knife like a sword. What makes it needful to mention a thing so obvious to us who have lived there is that Englishwomen sometimes resent, as degrading to their sex, the Oriental custom that makes the man stalk in front; whereas a little reflection would show them, when familiar with plain facts of this kind, that there are reasons for it honourable to human nature. It is not as a master that a man, who is a man, precedes a woman, or goes into war, or business, or politics; but as a pioneer, protector, provider, and in short head servant. The old maid, at whom Dean Ramsay made us laugh, because she "thought a man was perfect salvation," was moved by a wise inherited instinct, far different from what simple sophisticated persons have hitherto supposed.

On this occasion there was no man at all, and in the absence of any natural protector it was "go as you please." A tigress in the bush saw her chance. The lightest-limbed and lightest-laden of the trio was a little girl, Mintha by name, who ran on in front. The tigress seized her and carried her away.

There is a lot, at times, in etymology. An Englishman who knows Burmese would tell you that *Mintha* means prince, or son of an official (min); but, as written in Burmese, without a long accent on the *tha*, and pronounced like an ordinary English word with the stress in front, the name Mintha has another modest meaning which you may discover from a dictionary, but can only with difficulty persuade a Burman to tell you. It means *Better-than-an-Official*, a name curiously recalling the kind of names that were common in England in the great days of Cromwell.

"We know what judges can be made to do," said Selden, grimly.

"We know what officials are," the Burmans have been saying for centuries; and they class them with thieves and plagues, perhaps with more emphasis to-day than ever before. So Mintha is an unpretentious name, and so common that the little girl who bore it had probably never thought of the meaning of it, and would certainly have referred you to her mother if you had asked her about it.

She was perhaps eleven years old, but small for that age, this brown little maiden whom they called "Better-than-an-Official," and swift and silent like a dream the tigress stepped out and picked her up and carried her away between its teeth, as a cat does a little mouse.

Her older sister, Ngway Bwin, which means Silver-blossom, a girl on the verge of womanhood, about fourteen years old, was next behind her, and beheld her taken. She quickly turned to the third girl, Shway U or Grain-of-Gold, who happened at that moment to have a chopper in her hand; and, snatching the chopper, little Silver-blossom ran at the very top of her speed after the tigress. She overtook it, and lifting the big knife high above her head with both hands, she brought it down heavily on the animal's head. It dropped little Mintha, "Better-than-an-Official," and stood as if it were stunned. It was easy to see the need of keeping it stunned. Silver-blossom knew that that was her only chance. So hammer, hammer, hammer, cut succeeding cut, the little Burmese maiden killed the tigress.

Grain-of-Gold was the only other person near. She always said, and says still (1909), that she did nothing but look on. The village headman reported, and still reports, that the animal, which was shown to everybody in 1894, was a full-grown tigress in the prime of life, measuring "8 cubits and 2 meiks." A cubit, in rough village measures, is still the original cubit, from the elbow to the farthest finger-tip, and a "meik" is the width of a clenched fist with the thumb standing out. So 8 cubits and 2 meiks can hardly be less than 11 or 12 feet; but the villagers measure along the curved outline of the body, so we may conclude the straight measurement was 8 or 9 feet.

The soft brown skin of Better-than-an-Official had been broken and she was a little hurt on the back of the neck and on one arm; but these injuries were so slight that it is likely the tigress meant to give its cubs the pleasure of playing with her, instead of which Better-than-an-Official, saved by her sister and quickly cured of her scratches, is now reported to be living at Kule village, Mingin township. The sister, Silver-blossom herself, was quite unhurt. She became, deservedly, the pride of the countryside, but "died of a decline" ten years afterwards.

If her adventure appeared in a romance one would smile at the absurdity of the author who expected to be believed for a moment. Yet, after carefully questioning everybody concerned, Mr Tilly, who is a man of sense, believed it at the time and has never doubted it; and Mr Grant Brown, after a new local inquiry, believes it; and so do I. Let readers please themselves.

It may assist them to a right conclusion to remind them that Michelet has shown that Joan of Arc seems stranger to us than she really was because we are ignorant of history. Her performance was glorious for herself and France, one of the most glorious episodes in the history of the world; but all the same it was only the superlative of many similar doings of brave French women. Precisely in the same way it has to be remembered that, like hens emboldened to fly in the faces of dogs or boys in defence of chicks, many girls in charge of brothers or sisters have been known to surpass belief in their feats of devotion. So Silver-blossom was not odd in the sense of being peculiar. She was like other brave girls, only more so.

At the same time it would be wrong to minimise what she did. It is the exact truth to say she expanded the range of human possibilities. Think of a Burmese child doing that!

Let them who know no better "explain" the miracle. The man who ceases to wonder at it does not understand it. I frankly admire the girl, and have no "explanation," unless it be one to quote the hymn—

> "God moves in a mysterious way,
> His wonders to perform."

A pious Quaker's phrase would have been, "God moved her." If there is in

English any better name for the Living Spirit of the Universe that surged in her heart and nerved her arm, it is not known to me. But, as a good Muslim Imam of my acquaintance once remarked to me, "There are many names for God."

VI

THE OLD MEN AND THE TIGER

THIS was told me in 1908 by Mr Thomson, who as District Magistrate had held an inquest at the time upon the tragedy; and his recollections have been verified and supplemented by Mr Webb, the present District Magistrate. The depositions have, in ordinary course, been destroyed; but the details that are still recoverable seem to be sufficient.

The time was 1900, and the scene was Zwettaw village, Thongwa township, not far from Rangoon. The old headman, U Myat Thin, described in confidential official registers which he never saw as "an easy-going old Talaing" or native of Lower Burma, was sauntering outside the village about midday, watching his grandchildren, who were playing near him. Suddenly a tiger appeared and seized and carried away his grand-daughter. That kind of thing is done with the speed of thought; and Hercules himself, in the old man's place, could not have prevented the tiger getting the child. Probably Hercules himself, if unarmed, would have done no more than the old man did, namely, run into the village and shout for help.

But who was to help? Every man and woman fit for work was away in the fields. Only the old people and children were in the village. He took a spear from his house, and three other old men like himself did likewise. The four of them followed the tiger at once, and tracked and ran with such goodwill that they overtook him, though they were too late to save the child.

One of the finest traits of character which I have noticed in Burmese villagers is their readiness to fight to recover from a wild beast the body of any person it has killed. Let a European try to take a bone from a bulldog and he may be able to guess, faintly and distantly, at what these four old men were undertaking when they closed with a famishing tiger, to fight him for his freshly-killed food. They had no firearms, no missiles of any kind, not even bows and arrows. They had nothing to rely on but each other, as, with one spirit, they attacked him, thrusting at his vitals with their spears. The fight was too unequal. He killed one of them, and with a stroke of his paw he broke the shoulder of the grandfather, and so escaped away.

The news was sent to the men in the fields, and as soon as possible a new party took up the trail, including policemen with guns. They had not far to go. In the next field they found the tiger—dead. He had been gored to death by a herd of buffaloes that had been peacefully grazing there when he came among them.

If he had not been wounded they would probably not have attacked him, or he would not have lingered long enough to give them a chance. So the old men had not fought in vain.

A herdsman of experience has said to me: "If the tiger was bleeding, the sight of his blood would make the buffaloes charge him." That coincides with a red rag irritating a bull in England; but another herdsman said it was the smell, and several thought the wound made no difference. "A buffalo will not stand to be eaten by a tiger, but at sight of one stampedes, either at him or away from him." Very likely, indeed.

"I think the grandfather recovered," continued Mr Thomson. "I know I recommended a good reward and that it was paid." It appears from the official registers that he was quite well before the end of the year. On 12th December 1900 the Assistant Commissioner felt bound to note, as a matter of business: "The daily pilgrimage to the local Kyaung (a Buddhist monastery) is the end of his existence now, I think." Why not? In the heroic days of Greece a time of prayer was deemed the fittest ending to a well-spent life.

It was not till 29th June 1908 that the registers tell of him what has some day to be told of us all—"Deceased. For successor see ..."

So far as can be discovered, the brave old man paid no heed whatever to the rewards, or to what was thought about him. It was right to honour such gallantry in every possible way; but the deed was one no money could have purchased, and the story is one I like to tell whenever I hear anybody who knows no better talking of the "cowardice of the Burmans."

VII

RECOVERING THE CORPSE

THE present Deputy Commissioner of Pyapon district, Burma (Major Neth-ersole, 1909), is my authority for this incident, which is selected as the most re-markable of several of its kind. He investigated it on the spot, and told me of it at the time. He himself gave as many days as he could spare to hunting the tiger concerned, which killed eight men in Pyapon district before it met its fate.

One of them was old Po An, the headman of Eyya village. "Eyya" or "Irra" is the first part of the name of our local Mississippi, the Irrawaddy, and the village is, in fact, at the mouth of the great water-way so called, though it is only one of many water-ways through which the mighty river mingles with the sea. In other words, the village is on the coast, and about the middle of the delta, between Rangoon and Bassein.

In the last week of 1908 Po An and his son, and a friend of his own age (about sixty), left home together to get bamboos. They went in a little boat, landed where they intended, entered the muddy woods and cut what they wanted, and started to carry the bamboos to their boat.

They had heard that there was a man-killing tiger "somewhere thereabouts," but the Burman with a knife in his hand is not easily frightened in the forest. They made the mistake, which is the besetting sin of brave men and used to be called English, of despising the enemy, and did not even keep close together. In return-ing bamboo-laden, Po An lagged behind "about forty yards," but nobody thought anything of that. His son and companion heard a noise in the jungle too, but did not think of it till a minute or two later, when they ceased to hear the sound of Po An behind, and shouted, "Are you all right?" Receiving no reply they looked round. Not seeing him they laid down their burdens and retraced their steps, but had not far to go. In a glade through which they had come they saw the prostrate figure of Po An and the tiger standing over him.

They were only two men, and one of them was old, and they had no weapons but the big knives they had been using. But instantly they flourished their knives and moved forward, shouting and yelling as if they were the advance guard of an army of men.

The tiger, a big animal in the prime of life, looked up at them in deliberate surprise, and visibly hesitated. Then, as they approached, he moved aside, slowly and reluctantly, into cover, as if to watch what was going to happen and consider what to do.

The two men ran forward, snatched up the corpse and started for the boat, looking round continually, brandishing their knives and shouting, and seeing, or thinking they saw, those great eyes glaring at them through the bushes. They said they even heard the tiger following. Perhaps they did. Time after time they thought it was about to spring upon them, and faced towards the sound, real or imaginary, with knives uplifted and loud shouts of defiance. They reached the boat and got on board, but did not take time to loose the rope. They cut it and pushed off.

Next morning the elder of the two took Major Nethersole and another officer to the place, and there they saw the severed rope and the tracks of the tiger patrolling on the muddy banks. The tides had been such that the tracks must have been made after the men departed, and left no room for doubt that the tiger had come after them to the water's edge, and there lingered long, going up and down as if in a cage, and looking across the waters on which the men had disappeared.

It was several days before the son of Po An and his old friend discovered, as their excitement abated, how badly their nerves had been shaken. Their sleep began to be broken by hideous dreams.

That was more than three months ago. The tiger is dead now (April 1909). His skull and hide can be seen at Pyapon. But still, I believe, though now at greater and greater intervals, sometimes the one and sometimes the other of the two brave men is wakened by the nightmare of those awful eyes, and shrieks and shrieks to his neighbours to come and stay beside him.

VIII

THE INSPECTOR'S ESCAPE

IT was about February 1891, and on the left or eastern bank of the Sittang River in Toungoo district, Lower Burma, that an inspector of police was riding northwards along a cart-road, through the woods, as the daylight was quitting the sky, and "suddenly," to use his own words, "I seemed, at one and the same instant, to get a terrific blow in the small of the back, and to feel the pony under me springing upwards, as if it were jumping to the sky." He completed his description by gestures.

A listener suggested, "As if it were suddenly galloping up a wall?"

"Quite so," said he. "The next I felt was that I seemed to fall back upon something soft, and that's all I know. The next I saw was the people bending over me, and I could hear one say to another, 'He's not dead yet,' and others said, 'He's dead,' but none of them touched me, and I tried to speak, but could not. Then after a long time somebody saw I was breathing, and somebody put something under my head, and ... I am not hurt, so far as I am aware," concluded the inspector, "but feel stunned and queer, and horribly helpless."

The villagers said, "We saw the pony come galloping with an empty saddle along the road which goes through the village, and in the middle of the village it stopped short and made a noise. It was quivering. Its hind-quarters were bleeding from great tiger's claw-marks as you see them yet."

The poor beast was still sore from the scratches a month afterwards. Whether it ever recovered I never heard.

With a celerity and courage characteristic of the unspoiled Burman, every man in the village soon had a da (big knife) or home-made spear in his hand, and many had torches or lamps as well. But while they thus prepared for action promptly, it has to be noted that there was a certain hesitation about starting. Some objected. Why? The pony had been recognised as the inspector's. He was rather popular than otherwise, but he was a policeman. No Burman could say with truth that he thought it right to save the life of a policeman. Even the older men, who were addicted to religion, could only say, "He's a man, after all." Equally with the rest they believed that any policeman in the pay of the English is irretrievably doomed to hell, and has deserved to be. But, what made the pious elders on this occasion more readily silent than they might otherwise have been, there were several who delivered themselves of sentiments that might be translated by a verse of an old English ballad:—

> "Saddled and bridled
> And booted rade he;
> Toom hame (empty home) cam' the saddle,
> But never cam' he!"

"It's not a man that you're going to save. You're likely to be late for that! It's a corpse you're going to take from a tiger."

This was conclusive. The most scrupulous Burman can risk his life with a clear conscience in fighting a tiger to recover a corpse. So the crowd set out.

Great was their wonder to find the inspector prostrate upon the road, unconscious, but unscratched. When they had heard his story they said to me, —

"The tiger cannot have seen him at all. Lying in wait here, it must have seen only his piebald pony, and, leaping so as to land on its shoulders, it must have knocked its nose severely against the man's back and slipped down. Then he fell upon it, and so perplexed it more than ever, and it would step aside into cover to consider awhile."

Perhaps the shrewdest remark made on the incident was this: "When struck on the back, the man must have let out a howl. That would frighten the tiger!" The inspector did not remember that, but could not be expected to remember it. He would do it without thinking.

It was his own and the general opinion that if help had not come, as it did, the tiger would have come back; and, humanity mastering prejudice, the people said, "We are glad we came."

The fright made him talk of leaving the police and leading a new life. But his salary was good. He was like the rich man in Scripture, who had great possessions. The villagers did not blame him for changing his mind and not resigning. It was as much in earnest as in jest that they said, "He may become religious, when he takes his pension."

About the same time as this wonderful escape, a lonely leper who lived in a hut, like a hermit, on the opposite side of the river, disappeared for ever, and the few bloody rags that were left and the tell-tale footprints showed that the tiger had come upon him, like a thief in the night, and carried him bodily away.

"We are very sorry for the leper," said the villagers to the inspector, when he next rode by, and the fate of the leper was discussed. "We are very sorry for the leper, and for the tiger too. Either your pony or yourself would have been more wholesome eating."

IX

THE SOUND OF HUMANITY

THE leopard, if not the boldest of all the feline tribes, is at least the best acquainted with mankind. His partiality for dogs makes him familiar with men's villages. More than any other beast, perhaps, he is prompt to turn at bay when wounded and "charge home." Many a man has lost his life to a wounded leopard. Yet even a leopard is daunted by the sound of humanity.

In 1888 a big one was seen in a large village, not far from Maulmain, one morning. The scattered wooden houses and plentiful shrubs afforded cover. He was merely looking for a dog, and the people said he had repeatedly taken one unnoticed. But this morning a woman saw him and shrieked. The other women shrieked responsive, the children screamed, the dogs barked, and, amid the deafening uproar, the men of the village, and some chance visitors who happened to have guns, concerted measures, partly by dumb show, being scarcely able to make themselves audible to each other.

As soon as the men had obtained silence on one side of the clump of brushwood, wherein Mr Spots was waiting for the clamour to subside, and the men began yelling on the other sides of it, the leopard stepped cautiously into the open on the silent quarter, looking like a detected thief, preparing to run, with his tail between his legs, like a dog that feels he is about to be kicked and deserves it. On seeing an unexpected man in front of him, the leopard shrank aside, apologetically, as if abashed. The man killed it. A sense of what he owed to the other men prevented him allowing it to escape; and so he fired. But it was "against the grain." He felt like slaying a man who had asked for quarter; but, after all, no quarter is ever expected or given on either side in humanity's protracted war with dangerous cats.

In this case the leopard heard no shot until the shot was fired that killed it. It was cowed by the cries. So we need not wonder that the tiger, which is more sylvan in habit and less used to human noises, can be "beaten" out of shelter by the shouting of men and boys. When the tiger breaks out and kills a beater it is not because it has found the heart to face the yelling crowd, but because it is desperate.

We should remember that leopards and tigers love peace as much as do the Quakers. There is no jingo nonsense about them. They never want to fight, and absolutely will not fight unless they have to. Their single aim is to get their dinners, which, as Bismarck reminded a deputation, is the first business of every living being. "Good" or "bad" depends on the way of doing it, he might have added.

The war between cats and us is not due to their malignant hostility, but to their physiological necessities. If we were content to let them prey upon us there would be peace. On other terms there can be none. A compromise is impossible. What had to be settled, when the first Hercules took up his club, was whether the world was to be filled by men or cats. It is now some millenniums since the ultimate issue became obvious; but the end is not reached yet.

Of course it is not altogether an aversion to fighting that makes the tiger seek for peace at any price when men surround him. Try for a moment to think in the skin of a tiger. The little jungle dogs are formidable to him, as he is an individualist, and they run in packs. They kill the big deer before his nose, including some he has to leave alone. But what is the union of the dogs compared to the solidarity of men, who "have pity upon one another," as Mahomed noticed? And think again, what a puny thing is a tiger's tooth or claw compared to a big knife!

True it is that when a tiger finds a man unready and alone, he can kill him as easily as a man can kill a chicken. But in the course of ages he has acquired an instinctive horror of men, weak as they are, such as men, in turn, have of snakes. The unknown seems infinite, to tigers as to men. A dog has its teeth, a deer or bull its horns; but when a crowd of men are coming at him with a noise like a cyclone, a tiger cannot tell what to expect. So, even if you were a tiger, with a man's intellect to illumine the aspect of things in general, you would often feel along with it that the better part of valour is discretion.

It is not easy to think in the skin of a tiger. It is easier to realise the effect of the sound of humanity upon a tiger's nerves by watching him and the beaters. The matter is not one upon which there is any difference of opinion possible. This said, nothing perhaps could make the truth so palpable to happy stay-at-homes as a reminiscence I recently heard from a brave European officer who has had experience as a hunter.

For obvious reasons I will omit details that might enable others to identify him against his will. Suffice it to say, the scene was "in darkest Burma," and the time about the end of the nineteenth century.

"You know," said he, "the noise that the tiger makes in going through kaing grass."

But readers in general cannot know that. So it may be explained. In the woods the tiger glides gently, and steps unheard upon dry leaves a man could not touch without a noise. He realises the ideal of good children—to be seen without being heard. It is not that he likes to be seen. He is of a retiring disposition, and prefers to be unnoticed so much so that even if you frequent his haunts you are not likely to see him more than once or twice in a lifetime, though you may comfort yourself—if it is a comfort—by reflecting that he doubtless sees you oftener. He may be a neighbour of yours all his life; as a cub, he may be fed upon your cattle, and, as a grown-up tiger, help himself to the same, without once showing his face or letting you hear his stealthy step. He comes and goes like a thief in the night, and if by rarest chance he walks by day it is on silent pads more noiseless than the best of rubber tyres. But the kaing grass reeds in swampy parts of Burma grow thick and high. They are seldom less than a man's height, and sometimes so high as to overtop a man on horseback, and too thick for a dog to get through. When the tiger is hunting there he has to lie in wait by the sides of the paths. I hesitate to believe what is sometimes said—that he never is noiseless in the kaing—but the evidence is overwhelming that he often goes through it "as loudly as a cart," say some who have heard him, as they waited for him over a kill, or, in one instance, over a calf tied up as a bait.

"The noise is not the *same* as a cart's, only as loud. It seems to be unmistakable if once you have heard it," said the hunter, whose experience is to be told. "There is a crackling swish—swish, as he crumples up the reeds at every stride. Think of my feelings when I heard it again coming at me as I was walking back to camp along the narrow footpath, with the reeds towering above me, as if shutting out all help, to hide you and drown your voice. Oh, my God!" The man was speaking years afterwards, and shuddered still. "It made me feel queer, I tell you," he went on. "I was paralysed till I remembered what to do. Then didn't I howl, 'Thank God!' and yell! and swear! Somehow you don't recall, at such a time, what you say at church. The tiger might have digested me before I could have repeated a prayer. But every particle of profanity, English, Burmese and Hindustani, that ever was in my head came out then with a howl. I didn't care what it was if it made a noise."

The curious listener, on history intent, tried to refresh his memory by leading questions, but he positively blushed at the recollection, and was as shy as a girl. He proceeded:

"I kept it up, you know—I had to, although I heard the sound draw back a little. It's no joke to have to bluff a tiger in the kaing grass and in the dark, when you cannot see but know he can, and may have his eye upon you. I never stopped the noise. I felt he might spring upon me if it slacked for a second. And when I could not think of any other oath I struck up singing...." And, in short, he emerged from the darkness into the flickering glare of the camp-fire, yelling "Rule, Brittania!" much louder than he ever sang before.

X

THE TIGER AT THE RIFLE-RANGE

ABOUT 1891 a tiger began levying taxes on the little town of Shwegyin (Shwayjeen), in Lower Burma, where the Shwegyin river joins the big Sittang. The people were used to leopards, but tigers had ceased from troubling them so long that, as one said, "you might as well try to persuade us that the dead had arisen as that tigers had come back." As there had always been tigers in the adjoining mountains, and the forest spread over the country, and touched the town on every side but where the rivers ran, this prejudice would have been surprising, if it had not been so very human. It is hard to persuade men of what they do not like. The people of Shwegyin were not to be talked out of their comfortable security. No words could persuade them to look out for tiger, but the deeds of the beast itself gradually did.

Though tigers and leopards alike are earnest tariff reformers, their schedules differ in details, and as week succeeded week, and the dogs, so dear to leopards, were steadily neglected, and the invisible enemy, hovering around the herds coming home carelessly, anyhow, in the twilight, took calves and cows and bullocks, as they chanced to stray and offer themselves, in a style no Burman leopard ever tries, its capacity for great destruction was allowed to prove its greatness, and the most prejudiced of the local elders was at last candid enough to say, "I fear I may have to admit it to be a tiger when it is dead and I see it."

At a meeting of the Municipal Committee the president mentioned, adding the losses reported, that the depredations in three months amounted to more than half a year's taxes on the town. Like other oppressors, it destroyed a great deal more than it needed.

The members groaned in chorus, especially those who had cattle. But one who had no such possessions remained cheerful and broke the silence, saying, "It will die some day."

A fellow-member who had had losses glared at the speaker, who was remarkably obese, and said, "If the tiger only knew how much better eating some fat men in our town would make, he might be persuaded to change his diet. I wish he would."

"I never go out at night," said the obese one, hastily, growing grave, whereat the others laughed, and, recovering his composure, he continued: "Tigers come and tigers go, but the taxes go on for ever. When one official goes, another comes." Receiving the expected murmur of applause, he added, "That's what I was going to say."

It should perhaps be remarked that officials in Burma are proverbially classed with thieves and similar afflictions. We must remember that the civilisation of Burma is older than that of England, and should not be angry when the people there smile at those of us who are simple enough to suppose ourselves anything better than an expensive nuisance.

"Of two equal taxes," a Socratic member asked, "which do you feel the more—the first you pay, or the second?"

"The second."

"And the second or the third?"

"The third."

"And the third or a fourth?"

Then all became eloquent simultaneously, lest an addition to the taxes might be in contemplation.

The conclusion was unanimous that the last tax was ever the worst, and the tiger's inflictions the hardest of all to bear. This emboldened a sufferer to propose a levy, and municipal compensation to losers—a proposal which his fellow-members declared to be impracticable. There was no lack of sympathy when details were told. Even the obese member remarked, with unaffected emphasis, "I was very sorry for Mother Silver when she lost a cow." And another fatality was told, and another, and another. If they could have compassed the tiger's death by voting, it would have quickly died.

It did not die. A vote is seldom more than a good resolution. Deeds always need a doer. The most a vote can do is to ensure the worker elbow-room, and in this instance it was superfluous. Nobody wanted to spare the tiger. How to catch it was the problem. Its ravages were imputed to the English government, which had been confiscating arms. So the Deputy Commissioner lent guns and gave out ammunition gratis. But still the tiger flourished.

In vain did men spend nights in trees, "sitting up over a kill," as they expressed it. It never returned to cold meat. Why should it, with plenty of fresh cattle available? In vain did they study the ways it went, and sit in ambush. There was an infinite variety about it. It never repeated a catch in the same place and way. To describe completely all its doings, and the plans that *failed* to catch it, would fill a book.

At an early period of its history the people began to fetch the cattle home by daylight; but that simple device did not defeat it long. True, it loved the darkness better than the light, and the herds came home undiminished. But the tiger was not to be driven back to a lighter diet so easily. He followed his food. The cattle disappeared in the dark from pens and sheds, and tell-tale marks proclaimed that the thief was the enemy with four big legs and ugly claws.

At times there was an intermission of some weeks, long enough to let everyone grow careless again. But it had only gone to the hills, most probably as people go to Carlsbad, to rest its digestive organs. Then it returned to business with appetite refreshed, a very hungry tiger. People began to speak of it with bated breath and shows of humbleness, as an Englishman talks of a lord or a German of an emperor. That feeling grew to a superstitious dread. This was clearly more than an ordinary tiger.

"Perhaps it is a tigress with a litter of hungry kittens," was a matter-of-fact suggestion, received with a shudder, as if it had been disrespectful, a kind of lese-majesty. Besides, the suggestion was at last seen to be wrong, for once at last, once only, and then only after it had killed its scores, it was seen. A man was riding in the moonlight along the lonely boundary road, and saw it stride across the road, and sit down on the farther side, as if to wait to see him pass. It did not crouch. It sat up squarely, like a cat at home. It raised its head as high as possible, as if to enjoy the coolness of the evening breeze, which was as welcome to the tiger as to any European. On sight of it the rider's Arab mare began to dance, and turned again and again to bolt backwards. This saved Mr Stripes, for the rider, though apparently unarmed, had a pistol in his pocket, and had taken it out and was preparing to empty it as he galloped past. But the mare would not go nearer than 30 yards. The tiger became tired of watching her pirouetting, and stood up as if to depart. The rider fired, and at the sound of the shot, which missed, the tiger slouched swiftly into the woods unharmed, and gave no time for a second shot. When the man arrived at his house, a mile away, he found five other men at his gate, waiting for him, and saying, "Come with us. He" (there was no need to be more explicit) "is slaughtering now on the inner side of this road. We know where he'll cross it, and are going to ambuscade him."

"No use!" was the reply. "I have just seen him pass." They went to see if they had guessed aright. But no! The spot they meant to ambuscade was half a mile from the actual crossing-place.

Perhaps the only man in the town who had a gun and did not hunt that tiger was the Sergeant-Instructor, a solitary representative of the British army, stationed in Shwegyin to drill the volunteers. And the reason why he did not go a-hunting, as everybody knew, was that Mrs Sergeant-Instructor had announced that she would go with him.

She meant it too. "Another lady" in the station had sat up with her husband. Why should she not do likewise? If a tiger fight had been the kind of thing she supposed, such as might be shown in a circus or a tournament, she would have made a magnificent second to her gallant husband, and so he admitted. If only the tiger would come openly to their door in daylight, "instead of skulking in the dark round about, like a coward," as I believe she said, Mrs Sergeant-Instructor would have done her duty, and probably a good deal more. And she undoubtedly was disgusted with "the man's poor spirit." But every man in the station knew better. As an officer whispered to me: "What would be the use of the man sitting up with Mrs Sergeant-Instructor? She could not hold her tongue five minutes, not to speak of hours."

Nevertheless, there was chaff enough at first, which it was hard for him to bear until, in time, the continual failures of experienced hunters, magistrates and foresters, policemen and soldiers and others, became a consolation.

"Ah, the target is easier to see than a tiger," he would murmur, when scoring at the range.

The range was a clearing in the forest on low ground, upon the municipal boundary, a clearing of about 100 yards wide and 600 long.

One morning the Sergeant-Instructor went to it alone, with a rifle in his hand and two or three cartridges in his pocket. "As a kind of object for the morning's walk," he explained, "I meant to fire a shot at the range, to make sure I had got the rifle springs right. It was a bit stiff last Sunday. I had been working at it, to diminish the pull-off."

As you descend to the range from the main road, you first arrive at the 600 yards' station, the butts being at the farthest end; and this morning, "seeing all clear," said he, "I just lay down at 600 yards, and decided to take the shot from there, without going any farther.

"So I shifted about as usual, till I was lying comfortably, and adjusted my sights, and took aim; and then, just before pulling the trigger, I cast my eyes to windward, to the left as it happened, to see what the trees were like, and whether my allowance for the breeze was right. As I was looking at the trees on my left, I saw the tiger come out and walk across the range, to go between me and the target. I was glad there was nobody there. There was no time to talk. It did not hurry, so to speak, but went fast over the ground, fast and straight, like a man going to catch a train, with no time to lose, but too big a bug to run—you know the kind of thing."

"Like a man going over a level-crossing?"

"You might say that, but he did not look up and down. He stared straight in front of him, and I am sure he did not see me at all, or look to see anything on either side."

"Like the ideal Christian pilgrim, not looking right or left?"

The Sergeant seemed puzzled. He had not noticed anything pious about it. So I tried again.

"Like a dog after game? Perhaps he was after something?"

"That's it, that's it. I'm sure he had sport in sight."

"Preoccupied, so to speak?"

"Very much so. You know there are always cattle grazing on the far side of the range. He was hard at them. I just had time to shoot and no more. I noticed he would cross at 300 yards, and, doing everything as fast as I could, I lowered my sights, and aimed, and fired. He dropped, and never moved, and ... here he is...."

It had been a fine tiger, in the prime of life; and, as doctors say after a post-mortem, the corpse had all the appearance of having been extremely well nourished. Death was the result of a sudden failure of the heart's action, due to violence.

The Sergeant-Instructor had scored a bull's-eye.

XI

A LESSON FROM THE WATER BUFFALO

1. THE BUFFALO AND THE SKUNK

WHEN the Philippinos tell you now of the swagger of the Spaniards, which was the sorest of the sorrows that drove them into revolt, they often mention that the Spaniards called them "water buffaloes."

"To call you geese would have been kind in comparison?"

"Oh, quite polite!"

Indeed the water buffalo known to us in Burma, also, is not smart at all. Slow, heavy and dull, amphibious in his habits, he moves like a very fat pig, with almost less agility. Slipping through the muddy slush, in the sleekness of his prime, he looks almost "like a whale?" Yes, round enough for that, and almost like a little whale, except for his awkwardness, for his legs are not yet atrophied or sea-changed, and he has only his legs to move by; and also except—a big exception—his huge horns. These are extended like the arms of a gesticulating orator or other creature that flings his arms wide and turns up his hands; but never were arms flung out so gracefully as those horns, with a sweep like that of a scythe or scimitar, symmetrical and pointed. They lie on the back, when the owner lifts its nose to sniff the wind, harmless and out of the way, like a sword in its sheath. There is nothing ornamental about them, any more than about the Forth Bridge; and yet so beautiful is fitness that perhaps no bovine head has finer ornaments.

It always surprises one to see how cool the beast remains with these exclamatory horns. But it is these very horns that let him remain cool and at leisure in the haunted woods. From tigers down, all possible enemies are afraid of them. So the Burman water buffalo never needs to hasten; and, like a gentleman of independent means, not needing to exert himself, grows slow. His gait is dignified. His mind is dull.

This is not rhetorical conjecture, but natural history. Every healthy, living organism is harmonious, meaning all of a piece, such as men try to make their pictures and songs, and everything else they want to make well; and this particular collocation of cause and effect might be illustrated and proved by many modern instances.

Not to be offensive to our fellow-men, who in every country exhibit the same tendency; averting our gaze from all who are happy in "having something else than their brains to depend upon"; avoiding politics, which is a legitimate field of natural history, but obscured by vapours which make observation difficult, let us take the skunk—not meaning any kind of men, who are really miscalled skunks, for they have none of the beast's qualities but one, and in general have the nimbleness of rats—let us come among the animals and candidly consider the four-legged skunk.

He is a little beast, no bigger than a house cat, and lives, as puss would do in the woods, on worms and insects and mice and birds and such small game. But he is not nimble, like the cat, or fox, or any other hunting and hunted creature. He is as leisurely as the water buffalo, and as careless of observation in the wildest country as a dog in a farmer's yard. However hungry, the bigger beasts of prey, whose natural food he might seem to be, prefer to leave him alone. The fact is that he can make himself be smelt in a sickening way for nearly a mile off; and so "the skunk," according to an observer, "goes leisurely along, holding up his white tail as a danger-flag, for none to come within range of his nauseous artillery."

"Call me a skunk?" a man might say, "I wish I were, sometimes." There is perhaps no kind of life that is not worth living; so we need not wonder that there is something to envy in the skunk. The water buffalo is a perfect gentleman, compared to him; but the same security against enemies has produced in both the same leisurely habits. The horns protect the buffalo, and are at once his weapon and his danger-flag.

2. HUNTING THE BUFFALO

ON the last day of 1908, in a morning walk at Myaungmya, Lower Burma, I met two acquaintances, Messrs Dunn and M'Kenzie, riding home. They had elected to enjoy their Christmas holidays a-hunting, and been away for several days.

"Hunting what?"

"Buffalo."

"I believe the buffalo is a dangerous beast to tackle."

They looked at each other in a way that showed they had an adventure to tell. They had gone with another European and a crowd of followers to a muddy island in the delta, where a wild bull buffalo lived. They had failed to find him, and were all walking carelessly away, when he accidentally met them. The sight of a mob where he had lived alone, like Robinson Crusoe, startled the old bull, and he charged. Then magistrates, policemen and followers stampeded in many directions. With the instinct inherited from our forgotten arboreal ancestors, the fugitives sought refuge in the trees; but the trees were too small to lift them above the reach of the horns, and one or more would have been killed if Mr Dunn had not stumbled and fallen in the mud. This stopped the buffalo, which tried to pick him up, but could not do it, as he had the sense to lie flat. So it passed on; and Dunn then crawled to where his servant had dropped his gun, and recovered it, and shot the buffalo.

3. TAMING THE BUFFALO

THIS adventure shows how easily lives might be lost in hunting the wild buffalo, about which the herdsmen who know him best have told me what should, perhaps, be better known, were it only to prevent misunderstandings. There is not the slightest need for war between buffaloes and us. They are not natural enemies, like the tiger. They are not even troublesome to tame, like the deer.

"Though terrible to kill, they are easy to catch," say the herdsmen familiar with their haunts. "You have only to decoy them into a pen, and once there they can sell for a price at once, like those born in the village. They are more valuable," said one herdsman.

"But the taming?"

"That's nothing. Let them starve till they are weak. Then feed them up, slowly. Make them feel they are being fed by men."

"They can see that."

"No, for you generally bandage their eyes. You have to speak to them and not leave them to eat as if they found the food themselves. Let them know they owe it to you."

"You don't think of that at all," said another man. "Neither do they. This is what happens. There's generally a lot of them, like a herd. Some would be dead, before others were weak. If you just flung the food in anyhow, the weaklings would be the last to get it. You keep an eye on them, so as not to lose any; and whenever you see that one is weak, you feed that one."

"It comes to the same thing," rejoined the man who spoke first. "They learn that men are their friends, and then they'll do anything you want."

"Do they work willingly?"

"Who ever did? They do what they have to, like other people. A buffalo is so mighty that he hardly needs to make an effort to pull the plough. The one new caught and tamed does as well as the rest."

"Why is he worth more?"

"He isn't," said the other man, quoting figures. An argument followed, and in the end they agreed. A newly-tamed herd might sell for less per head than village-born cattle, if the wild ones caught included more old animals and calves. Compare contemporaries, and the wild one is the better.

"Why?"

Various reasons were suggested, including one that was oddly expressed. "The wild animal is the more vigorous, because he has never been spoiled by working. Think how different I would have been if I had never had to work for my living!"

This was absurd. Till we came here, with our commercial creed that money makes the man, education in Burma was universal and free to the poor, and, however it be in England, where factory workers breed in slums and breathe polluted air, in Burma the working man lives mostly in the fields, and is sturdier, and often more sensible, than the idler. The herdsmen reluctantly admitted this; and it led to a digression.

In a Socratic way, I explained the gospel of work, with half-and-half acceptance as long as I quoted only Chinese maxims and examples; but, happening to hint that the English also had that to teach the East, I spoiled the lesson. There was a general laugh. "When do the English work?" Then one asked the other: "Did you ever see an Englishman working?" They said to each other that the only Englishmen who worked were one or two, whom the others did not speak to, but treated like the Pagoda-slaves of native Burma. We returned to the buffaloes.

"Why is the wild one the better?"

"He is stronger, and fresher, and quieter."

"Quieter?"

"Yes. He thinks of men, women and children as his feeders, and will never hurt anybody, and a little child can lead him."

"A child can drive the village cattle."

"The wild ones tamed are safest of all." (It should be noted that the domestic buffalo is dangerous occasionally, and people are sometimes hurt or killed by them.)

"Don't they notice that men caught them?"

"They're not clever enough for that."

"Don't they try to escape?"

"Never. Why should they? They have all they want. It is our business to keep them contented, and it's easy."

"Their calves are at times obstreperous," a man added, after a pause, and the others agreed, but said, "All you need do, at the worst, is to cut their horns, that is, cut off the tips."

"Why not do that to all the calves? There's somebody killed or hurt by buffaloes every year in Burma."

"The glory of a buffalo is his horns. It would be wrong, because it would not be natural to blunt them. We would never do it unless we could not help it, when a particular beast is bad."

"It's too much bother, I suppose."

"No, it's easy. But it does not look natural. The buffalo with his horns blunted is disfigured, and seems to feel it."

"No, no, it's not natural at all," said one after the other, with emphasis.

"How do you hunt the buffalo?"

"We never hunt the buffalo. No Burman ever did. At any rate, none ever does now. It is much safer and easier to catch and tame them; and it pays better."

A buffalo went by as our talk was ending; and on its withers was sitting a little boy of six or seven years of age, drumming merrily on its broad neck with his heels. At sight of us, he signified to it, by slaps and shouts, to move aside, so as not to splash us; and the big buffalo gently obeyed.

XII

THE BUFFALO AND THE CROCODILE

WHEN the rains have all run off, and the snows of Central Asia have not begun to melt, about the middle of the dry weather, the Irrawaddy, our Burman Mississippi, runs its lowest; and in such places as Magwe, a district on the road to Mandalay, the sandbanks are conspicuous. In 1894 there was, as there often is, a sandbank in Magwe district that, starting from the eastern bank, like a dam, athwart the current, bent down the stream, like a breakwater at sea, enclosing a natural harbour between it and the bank. This little harbour was shoaled at its southern or open end by the silting sands in the water eddying there; but for most of its length it was deep enough to be as comfortable for the cattle as if the whole enclosure had been made for their convenience.

It was all a big buffalo-wallow one afternoon that year (1894). One after another, scores of long-horned buffaloes had subsided into it, like submarines, leaving little but their nostrils on the surface. Men and women stood about on the bank, and children were bathing at the water's edge. Suddenly a splashing drew all eyes. It takes much to excite a buffalo. Even their manner of fighting is more than elephantine. I stood and watched a duel among them lately (1908), but never will again. It was perhaps the most leisurely battle that human being could endure to watch. But there, in 1894, men stared in wonder at a huge cow-buffalo splashing distractedly southwards from the extreme upper end of the pool. They soon saw she was chasing a crocodile that was carrying off her calf. Finding herself distanced in the water, she took to the shore, and galloped like a cart-horse in a hurry.

"I don't know," said an onlooker, "whether we could have reached the shoal in time to be of any use, but when we saw the old cow going like that, we thought it best to stand aside."

This was wise. The buffalo is enormous, and might easily kill a man by inadvertence, and a big crocodile, such as they said this was, though not so overwhelming, is otherwise dangerous. It does not seem to have been ascertained how old a crocodile can be. It seems to live to a great age, once it passes safely through the dangers of adolescence, and to continue growing bigger the longer it lives, like a tree. In Arakan I had seen some Indian coins that had ceased to be current for about a century, and were then, in 1893, recovered from the stomach of a patriarchal crocodile. The likeliest guess was that he had got this trouble in his stomach—for such it probably was to him—by eating one of the corpses that furnished such plenteous feeding to his tribe in the wars in Arakan, more than a century before.

There was nothing certain, of course, except the age of the coins and the fact that they were found in his stomach, and he might have eaten another beast that had eaten the corpse, or he might have recently dined upon an Arakanese archæologist, but it is at least as likely that he had been suffering—if he suffered—a hundred years, for the headlong gluttony of youth.

A Sanskrit proverb runs:

> When lion and striped tiger fight a bout,
> It's best to leave these two to fight it out.

So the Burmans felt as they watched the march of events:

> When buffalo and crocodile debate,
> The thing for man to do is—stand and wait.

They had not to wait long.

"It was the nicest thing I ever saw in my life," said a man to me, his voice almost trembling with enthusiasm months afterwards. "I never heard tell of a thing like it. She went along the bank like a dog, in spite of her size. We ran to see better. Some say she made for the water, when she came abreast of the crocodile, but seeing the crocodile go by, drew back and galloped on again. I did not see that. We all saw the finish. She took the water at the shoal and stood waiting, like a cat. Of course the cattle knew the place, but fancy the old cow reflecting that the crocodile would need to cross the shoal to reach deep water.

"At first, while she stood waiting, we thought she was too late, as the enemy had gone below the surface, but soon we saw the stiff-necked crocodile, not looking round, slowly dragging the calf and itself over the sand, in front of the old cow. Ha, ha! She waited for the right moment, just like a cat; then charged, like a buffalo; and then we saw the great crocodile wriggling high in the air, spitted and tossed as easily as if it had been only a puppy. The horns both went clean through the middle of its body, and came out again."

I forget the fate of the calf, but they told me the taste of the crocodile's flesh. The nicest bits were near the tail. So I know that the crocodile died.

XIII

A NEST OF CROCODILES

IN 1893 and 1894 I was Deputy Commissioner of Kyaukpyu district, which means the islands of Ramri and Cheduba, and smaller isles adjoining, and an adjacent strip of the malarious coast of Arakan. The headquarters was in the north of Ramri, and, sitting in my house there, one evening early in 1894, I heard an unusual clamour at the door. There was audibly somebody having an altercation with my servants.

I went to see and hear. It was a fisherman from a far-off corner of the district. Till shortly before then the Government had paid rewards for the destruction of crocodiles and their eggs; and so this man, on finding a nest of crocodile's eggs, put them in a bushel basket and started with it for headquarters. He was nearly there before he heard that these eggs were no more paid for. Loath to lose his labour, he finished his journey and tried to sell them in the bazaar. There was a sensation. He had to run.

The people cried to him that he must not sleep in the town till he got rid of them. "Fling them into the sea," they said; but he was most unwilling. "Hope springs eternal in the human breast." Perhaps it was a lie that rewards were no longer paid? One never can tell what to believe. He decided to try to speak to the Deputy Commissioner before flinging the eggs away.

I heard his story, and told him it was true that rewards were paid no more; but I pitied the man and bought the nest from him, basket and all, paying him liberally. It is needful to mention the liberality of the payment to explain what followed.

"Take it upstairs."

The servants were men, of course, not women; yet they shuddered and drew back, each pushing another forward.

"I'll carry it for you!" cried the happy fisherman; "is it into the bedroom you want me to take it?"

"Put it on the front verandah."

The servants surveyed it from a distance. The eggs were in colour like hen's eggs, and about twice the size. They were longer, but hardly at all thicker, and peculiar only in being of the same size at both ends. Some scores of them were embedded in mud, with roots of reeds and grass; but there is no reason to suppose, as has been done, that the crocodile which laid the eggs had mixed the grasses with the mud. How could she, stiff-necked as she is, and unhandy? The mud so mixed would be the readiest available where the eggs were laid, between wind and water in a shallow tidal creek. That was where the fisherman said that he found them. The heat of the sun is what hatches them. Part of the day they lie bare to it or almost bare, and for the rest of the time they are covered by water which the sun has warmed. In such an incubator the heat of the rotting grass would matter no more than a lucifer match in a furnace. Of course, all life does hang upon the sun, but the unhatched crocodiles depend on it directly, and might make out a better title to celestial parentage than anyone I know, not even excepting the Emperor of Japan.

The servants remained alarmed. It was probably at their instigation that a carpenter came to see if he was not wanted to make a wooden wall to screen the verandah where the eggs were from the rest of the house. When bidden make anything he liked, if willing to be paid for it by two or three young crocodiles, he hastily retreated. The beasts have a bad name in Arakan. There, as in Egypt, they do eat people occasionally, but there is nothing else against them.

Another device of the servants was to keep the dogs beside the nest and feed them there. "To give us warning when the crocodiles come out," they said, "so that we may let you know." There was no doubt that the little dears were on their way—too far on their way to let me blow any of the eggs successfully. I did blow one or two, but the holes made by the departing contents were too big. The shells were not worth keeping.

The dogs were not needed after all. A number of visitors were sitting and standing around the nest on the morning when the great moment came, and the eggs atop began to open like popcorns. From every opening shell there leapt a baby crocodile, span-long but perfect, as nimble as a rat and desperately hungry. No wonder! Think of the food they needed to swell them to the size of their mighty parent.

It was difficult to study them. Whatever noise they made was drowned in the clamour of the visitors and servants; and they themselves, to the number of about half a dozen, were soon drowned in whisky, as the best substitute for the spirits of wine which had not arrived. Their little corpses may still be seen in Glasgow Museum, I suppose. At least, I sent them to it for a sepulchre. The rest, and all their unhatched brethren, found a more common grave in a hole that was ready for them in the garden.

I was very sorry to have to do this; but I had to be at office at 10 a.m., and if this had not been done before I went, I would have found my house desolate on my return, and no dinner ready. My servants would have fled unanimously. So the poor little crocodiles had to die. But it was humanely done, and the unhatched eggs were broken before being buried, and the earth rammed tight.

"Stand and see the man does it," I said to the "boy" or factotum.

"You may be sure it'll be done," said he, and added, with unusual cheerfulness, "we'll all be helping him."

Though the lucky fisherman had been told to say as little as possible, he had boasted so much of his good fortune that a plain-spoken vernacular proclamation had to be sent in all directions to this effect—

NOTICE
NESTS OF CROCODILES' EGGS

The Deputy Commissioner Does not Want any More

There was a curious sequel a month or two later. Somewhere about the south of Ramri Island, there lived a secluded farmer of strong intellect, who asked himself, "Why did the Deputy Commissioner want to hatch crocodiles' eggs?" His neighbours were asking themselves the same question, and to an interested gathering at a Buddhist temple he explained his solution of the conundrum.

"Why do we hatch the eggs of fowls? Because we want fowls. Therefore it must have been because he wanted crocodiles that the Deputy Commissioner bought and hatched the crocodile's eggs.

"He probably did not know, as we do, that the new-born crocodiles are untameable, like fishes. They need a great deal of time to grow big. But a full-grown crocodile is a very sagacious as well as a very hungry animal, and it would quickly become devoted to anybody who fed it as well as he could afford to feed it. So, if he paid so much for the eggs, he would give thousands of rupees for a really big and mature crocodile, especially if it were nicely tamed."

The wisdom of this reasoning was much admired. So the wise fellow and his friends sought the acquaintance of the dwellers in the creeks, and decoyed into a little tank a patriarchal crocodile. Some weeks were spent in "taming" it (and dosing it with opium, as was afterwards suspected). Then half a dozen men, no longer young, shouldered the pole to which the crocodile was tied, and carried it, more than a day's journey, to the district headquarters.

They came to the house of the Deputy Commissioner about the middle of the second day after leaving home, and were told he was at office. They went to seek him.

He was on the bench, in court. Shrieks and shouts and a wild stampede of people was the informal announcement of the new arrival. They stopped all business; but nothing stopped them. Not knowing the way very well, they began by entering the Treasury. The sentry shouted and the guard turned out with fixed bayonets and loaded rifles, in case this might be a manœuvre for more easily rushing the Treasury.

"We are fetching a live crocodile to the Deputy Commissioner," cried the newcomers to all who would listen to them. Then it was supposed they might have been sent for, and they were directed to the court-rooms.

The bailiff rushed into court, and, looking distracted, trembling and hardly able to articulate, he said,—

"Six men, with a great struggling crocodile alive, on the verandah now, coming in, nothing can stop them. They want to see the Deputy Commissioner. I went for the Superintendent of Police, but he is out. They won't listen to me."

I went out to them and had the beast carried downstairs, and heard their story.

There was no possible room to doubt their good faith. Their dream of a fortune, for such they expected, seemed like the Arabian Nights.

I told them I did not want a crocodile, but that as they had taken so much trouble I would pay them out of my own pocket, for killing it, the largest reward that Government used to pay. This was like offering a pound or two to men who looked for thousands. Of course they did not thank me. I left them to finish the matter themselves, and returned to business.

I was not to be quit of the crocodile so easily. For more than an hour a crowd continued to collect round the live monster as it lay on the grassy sands between the court-house and the sea. Then the bailiff returned to me more distracted than ever.

"The men have decided to unbind the crocodile and leave it where it is, and depart. They say they will not accept money as the price of blood. This is a tamed crocodile. It is like a friend. If it is dangerous now it is only because it is hungry. So long as it is well fed it will hurt nobody. They are not damned fishermen, nor damned hunters." (These adjectives were not used profanely, but correctly, as it is the popular belief that fishermen and hunters are damned.) "These men say that they are respectable Buddhists and cultivators. They would not kill a wild crocodile, much less a tame one."

"Put it in the sea."

"I told them to do so, but they said it wouldn't go."

"Bid them carry it to the creek a mile away."

The bailiff asked whether the reward was to be paid if it were let go in the creek, and thinking of possible damage subsequently I answered "No."

He returned to say, "The men declare that they have carried it far enough already. They've done enough for nothing."

"Then leave it bound."

"They want their ropes and pole."

"I'll take its blood upon my head. Call a man from the Treasury guard to shoot it. Let them fling its carcass into the sea and pay them then."

To this they agreed, it was reported; and, fearing some accident to the crowd, in the absence of the Superintendent of Police, I went to see the killing rightly done.

There was difficulty in getting people to move out of danger. So one of the men knelt beside the crocodile unbidden, and, with a knowing look, full of suppressed fun, he cut the strings that held the jaws together and some of the other ropes.

Slowly the crocodile moved and opened wide the greatest mouth I ever beheld—something suggestive of the "Jaws of Hell." The crowd shrieked and dispersed to a distance. Then the crocodile died. His bearers received the promised money, the fishes ate his body, and his blood is upon my head.

XIV

USEFUL SNAKES

IN the backwoods of Thayetmyo district, Burma, in 1886, I was next to the man who was guiding a party of policemen and villagers going, in single file, on the track of robbers in arms, who had been cattle-lifting. Suddenly the guide in front held his hand behind his back as a signal to stop, and I passed on the signal.

The guide began to move forward, on his toes, as noiselessly as a cat, towards something on the ground. His eyes were riveted upon it, 20 or 30 feet in front of him. To the rest of the party it was invisible. The only noise was the flick of a hand on a pony's neck, removing a horsefly; and even that was stopped, and all was hushed. We seemed to hold our breath, and, though the guide was moving as quick as man could move without a noise, he seemed to be creeping slowly, slowly. He lifted up his arms as he came near his object, and then dived forward, so to speak, not losing his balance, but taking a great step and stooping, and recovering himself with equal speed. Then we saw his game. He had caught by the tail a long snake, 5 or 6 feet long, and was whirling it in the air.

It was thrilling to see it writhing in vain resistance to the laws of matter and the tendency called centrifugal. Its wriggling ended after two or three thwacks of its head upon the ground; but, long after it was as limp as a whipcord, he went on twirling it and thwacking it. He reminded me of the Scottish motto, "I mak' siccar," or "I make sure." The legend is that when Bruce had stabbed a traitor at Dumfries and said to a henchman, "I think I have killed him," the henchman answered, "Think? I mak' siccar," and went and finished the killing. Our guide was as resolute as he to make sure; but after a while he held the limp thing at arm's length, and let it dangle a second or two in front of him, undeniably dead. Then he flung it over his shoulder and walked on in silence.

"Any use?" I cried.

"Curry for us all," he answered, looking backwards over his shoulder and seeming surprised at the question.

In 1887, a few months later, being on the Pegu Yoma Mountains between Toungoo and Thayetmyo, still on the same kind of business, and leading a crowd of hungry men, I remembered this, and shot a python more than 7 yards long and as thick as a man's thigh. We met each other accidentally, he and I. He had been dozing after dinner, and yawned in the finest old Piccadilly style. I sent an unmannerly bullet into his mouth, which killed him. For two days, at least, his flesh supplied the wherewithal to flavour the rice of more than forty men; but I cannot tell the taste of it. I have eaten silkworms curried. They tasted like shrimps. But if the reader wishes to realise the savour of snakes, let him eat them himself.

XV

THE TUCKTOO

BURMA is chiefly remarkable for a lizard that occasionally haunts the trees and houses there. Span-long or more, it has a head big out of all proportion compared with others of the lizard clans, and eyes that sometimes seem to follow you like owl's eyes, and a loud voice. "Tuck-too!" it cries, "Tuck-too! Tuck-too!" without any variation, except an occasional repetition of the "oo-oo-oo" at the end, like a musician tuning his pipes.

It is considered very lucky to have such a lizard in your house; and as it is said to be fond of baby rats, and rats bring plague, the prejudice may have some foundation in fact. Its principal food is insects—a wholesome appetite too; but its great glory comes from the similarity of its cry, weak in consonants and loud in vowels, to the Burmese for *Quite so*. It is a great prophet. They say the rains can be foretold by counting its *Quite sos*; and if you are about to wed you should ask it, "Is she good? Is she bad?" "Quite so, quite so," says the prophet, impartial as Fate. But perverse, let it stop first; and if your last question to get "Quite so" is the question,—"Is she bad?" you should break off the marriage. They say that marriages have been broken off on this account; and assuredly, in many a village, you can see and hear the children with mock gravity keeping time to the tucktoo and crying in chorus,—"Is she good? Is she bad?"

Sometimes, like other prophets, it comes to church to speak, never to listen; and then it may be loudly heard, to the joy of the congregations rather than of the clergy. The rest of its history has been embalmed in a song by one of its friends:—

I

There's a goggle-eyed cherub, that's living with me;
'Tuck-too! Tuck-too!'
And, whatever I do, he is anxious to see.
'Tuck-too! Tuck-too!'

II

With a crocodile's shape, but, thank Heaven! he's small,
'Tuck-too! Tuck-too!'
He walks on the ceiling, and walks on the wall
'Tuck-too! Tuck-too!'

III

When he opens his jaws, of a terrible size,
'Tuck-too! Tuck-too!'
I can hardly believe he's just hunting for flies.
'Tuck-too! Tuck-too!'

IV

His head's twice as big as it should be, at least—
'Tuck-too! Tuck-too!'
He's only a lizard as man is a beast.
'Tuck-too! Tuck-too!'

V

His cousin Chameleon keeps changing in hue;
'Tuck-too! Tuck-too!'
But he never alters, the steady Tuck-too!
'Tuck-too! Tuck-too!'

VI

By day and by night, he will tell you his name—
'Tuck-too! Tuck-too!'
And though he speaks often, it's always the same—
'Tuck-too! Tuck-too!'

VII

Yet there's many great speakers more tiresome than he,
'Tuck-too! Tuck-too!'
My goggle-eyed cherub, that's living with me!
'Tuck-too! Tuck-too!'
'Oo—oo—oo—oo!'

XVI

THE KITTEN'S CATCH

HE is a common grey kitten; but he is the last of a large family, and his mother is devoted to him, and takes great pains about his education. Now that he can run about, his mother fetches indoors little field-mice for him, and baby rats from the stable; and so the kitten is quickly learning the trade of all his tribe. But mother was digesting last night (11/6/09) and would not run about with him, would only flick her tail; and chasing mother's tail became gradually monotonous for a kitten that had had a field-mouse in his paws, to say nothing of a baby rat.

So he went and spoke to the big fat frog that was sitting in the corner of the dining-room, face to the wall, like a pupil at school sent to stand in the corner as a punishment. Only, the frog was not being punished. He was catching flies. He looked round at the kitten coming near and trying to draw attention. He is a pot-bellied frog, of elderly look, so that his leaping seems out of character. On this occasion, however, his deportment was unimpeachable. He looked at the kitten earnestly, but never spoke, moving nothing but his head, as he turned it round to see him. He gazed at the importunate little cat, as once a gaitered bishop gazed at a newspaper-boy who wanted to speak to him, but seemed unlikely to be polite. "I wish no ill to you, but please leave me alone." That was what the frog's look seemed to say; but he uttered no sound. Perhaps he thought that talking might disturb the flies he was catching, just as the gentle angler sometimes prays for silence, lest a whisper be heard by the fish.

The kitten took the hint and jumped upon a chair and thence to the table, and walked across it towards me. He is fond of me; that is to say, he sometimes comes to me when he has nothing else to do or wants something. But on the way across the table he saw what seemed more interesting. The brass Egyptian finger-bowl caught his eye, and he surveyed it and its doily. He had passed it unconcerned a few minutes before, but that was when preoccupied about the frog. On this occasion, after an attentive survey of the finger-bowl, he put out his paw and tried to push it sideways. It did not move. He tried a spring and a push, to add momentum to his muscle; and so he shook it a little.

He raised himself to his full height and looked and beheld something inside it, moving! Then he became excited.

When you try to think like a cat, you must begin by realising that he has fewer categories than Aristotle. The universe is, in his mind, divided into—*himself* and other things not-himself, which is exactly the feline counterpart of Hegel & Co.'s

Ego and Non-Ego; but, having to find a living, the cat has passed as far beyond the Hegelian stage as the Germans themselves have done since Hegel died. He classifies things not-himself into the Eatable and the Not-Eatable; and again, a cross-division, into what he fears and what he does not fear; and thirdly, another cross-division, he distinguishes things that move from things that do not move. Few hunting animals are long of learning that last distinction; and yet to know that motionless things escape the eye is one of the first lessons that scouts have to be taught. The kitten knew it. He flopped down motionless a while, as soon as he saw something moving inside the bowl; but men who have been miseducated into believing without observing, whose minds have been constricted by Greek grammars and the rest, as the feet of Chinese ladies are constricted by bandages, men of bandaged brains, in short, still need to be taught that in their maturity. Better late than never!

Stealthily the kitten now approached the bowl and tried in vain to jerk out what was inside. The bowl was too heavy for him. He crept round and round it, and endeavoured to move it by pulling the tablecloth, but failed again. Then he sat down at a distance, with his head between his paws, and watched it and considered, concentrating his intellect upon it, exactly as a boy sits down, with his arms round his head to puzzle out a thing, retiring into himself, so that distracting sights and sounds be held aloof, and only the problem to be solved find access to his brain. It is an excellent thing to make a *camera obscura* of your skull in that way at times. I have watched a great inventor doing it; and with like admiration I now watched the kitten. No apology is needed to my Brahman friends for mentioning that this concentration is what they call "Yoga," described as "a discipline whereby the powers in man are to be so trained that they will attain their utmost development, and will realise and respond to the subtlest and minutest influences which bear on him from outside." Such is ever the way of the wise; and it may be attempted by the simple too, if they are sincere. It is conceit and affectation that make the fool. The kitten had no weakness of that kind. So he meditated to some purpose; for he saw what to do.

He put out his paw and tugged the doily. Hurrah! The bowl moved briskly. The hunt was up now at the fifth tug the water flew out. The triumphant kitten darted round the bowl to catch his prey and found nothing. The tablecloth was wet; but how could he connect the wetness of the tablecloth with the thing that had leapt from the bowl?

I tried to console him with milk, but he was transported beyond the reach of sordid comforting. Besides, he was not hungry. He returned again and again to investigate the matter, till he was tired. Where had the thing gone to? He never guessed, and I could not tell him. Poor little puss! For him, as for humanity, the ocean of mystery, on which all things swim, is very close at times.

XVII

THE LEOPARD AS A KILLER OF MEN

1. TWICE TWENTY YEARS AGO OR MORE

NOT long ago I read in Indian papers about a leopard in Central India which had killed about 173 men and women, and the carcass of which showed fore-paws and chest muscles of unusual size. "It had almost the front of a tiger," wrote one of the scribes. This was exactly the description of another of the same kind, which was told me about 1888 by Colonel Bingham, then Conservator of Forests for an eastern division of Burma. He beguiled the long evening in a rest-house on the fringe of the woods by telling me the life-history of a man-killing leopard in Central India, which I believe he had hunted there about twenty or thirty years before. It made the "hours and minutes hand-in-hand go by" so light that it was long, long after our usual bed-time before we thought of looking at our watches.

If he had been the common story-teller, I could never have kept awake, much less forgotten to note the time. He was a man of accurate and scientific tastes, and great knowledge of Natural History, and, best of all, one of those rare comfortable souls who are more interested in things in general than in themselves. This makes accuracy almost easy, and modesty comes without an effort. We discussed at length the question whether that leopard had been a cross between the leopard and the tiger. The reports about it had made Bingham think it must be so, but the post-mortem upon it, at which I think he assisted, made him dubious, for, to his surprise, he found its markings purely leopard's, and the only difference between it and common leopards to be its size, especially in front.

"After all," I said, "the size is the chief difference between leopards and common cats." Bingham agreed, and I found he was still of the opinion that lions and tigers, leopards and jaguars, are all more nearly related than at first sight appears. He had been, as I then was, sanguine about getting evidence that they interbred, and while telling me he had never succeeded, thought another might. Indeed it should be better known that the chief difference between lions and tigers is the lion's way of wearing his hair. The difference in bone and muscle is less, much less than there is between varieties of domestic cats; and it is easy to exaggerate the specific importance of colour. I know a worthy Dutchman (Mr Hegt), who told me he acquainted Charles Darwin with an interesting accouchement of a lady-leopard in Holland. She brought forth at a birth kits black and white, such as the naturalists had till then classed as different species. Darwin was delighted at the news.

The best part of our talk, however, was about the leopard's adventures. Bingham was not a man to forget that the carcass cut up after death is not the leopard. It is merely a confused conglomerate of hide and flesh and bones and teeth and claws, drenched in blood. Such things are the mortal remains of the leopard; but its spirit, the fire of life that made it terrible, that great reality, whatever you call it, has fled away on the wings of the wind. So fled the spirits of its victims. Its fleshy garment lies before you as helpless as ever were theirs, as harmless as if it had been a sheep.

It was a little playful kitten in the forests, not long before it became a terrible killer of men, for its tribe grows fast. It took to killing as its trade, like a fish to water. Its mother taught it nothing else. When her milk ran dry, she taught it how to flesh its baby fangs; and under her kind, encouraging, maternal eyes it grew up big and strong, and then it left its mother's lair to feed itself and live alone.

There is something thrilling in the strangeness which such separation brings. The cat is a tender mother, but she soon forgets her children. A few months after parting, if this leopard and its mother met in the woods, they would glare at each other like strangers, without recognition. If you doubt this, study your civilised domestic cats, especially when they are hungry. The matter is not doubtful.

This does not mean that the leopards eat each other. As hawks do not peck out the eyes of hawks, so leopards seek for tenderer beef than that of leopards. Besides, their single aim in life being to satisfy their appetites cheaply, to risk a scratch would be bad business. So they compete in the woods exactly as mercantile firms do in the city, each grabbing all it can. They generally die of starvation, but see nothing odd in that. They have faced starvation all their lives; and even when the mother-leopard comes to perish so, there is no bitterness in her heart at the thought that it is her multitudinous kittens that have made food scarce. She has forgotten them. They have passed out of her mind completely, like the shadows of the clouds that pass across the surface of a mountain lake, and go by and leave no sign.

2. A LEOPARD THAT LOVED THE LADIES

COLONEL BINGHAM had not been able to ascertain what made this leopard take early to humanity. A guess that many favoured was suggested by its life-long preference for women. The guess was that its mother had given her little ones some girls to flesh their baby fangs upon. There had been some horrible cases of that sort. One shudders to think of girls in the maws of leopards, like the little mice a tabby brings to her kittens. But, after all, many a girl meets a worse fate in a European town. The human beast of prey is crueller than any cat.

Whatever the explanation, the fact, at which the Central Provinces of India soon were shuddering, was that this great leopard grew into a man-eater, that seemed to combine the strength and stomach of the tiger and the wily familiarity of the leopard. He took girls for choice. Of two women returning with water from the well, the one was taken and the other was left, that is to say, ran screaming home. So marked was his preference for their sex, that whenever he was supposed to be near a village, the women all became like purdanishin ladies, and would not go out of doors.

I believe it was a police-officer, but it may have been a "man in the forests," who told Bingham of being bothered by a nasty smell in a mango grove in which he had pitched his tent. They searched far and near for the cause of it a long time, and at last discovered the putrid half of a woman's body, hidden in the foliage, in a fork of a mango tree. The villagers said they knew by what was left that it was the remains of the leopard's meal, for it had an Homeric appreciation of entrails. The head was wanting, and the arms too; but the legs were little more than nibbled. About half the corpse had been put aside for further recourse, if needed. It had not been needed. The leopard must have found another. Indeed, they said that it seldom needed to dine upon cold meat.

It would often have had to do so, of course, if it had limited itself to women; but it no more thought of that than an epicure thinks of restricting himself to turtle. The women were its tit-bits; but they were so shy that it might often have starved if it had taken nothing else.

Its taste for them has often been discussed, but none of the theories propounded were more than guesses. The most interesting incident mentioned in these discussions concerned a leopard in the Shan States of Burma. It ordinarily lived on dogs and game and cattle, like other leopards, but once it killed a man and a woman. The magistrate who went to seek the corpses told me that, in following the trail, ornaments the woman had been wearing were found in bits on the ground, and then the two corpses—the man's untasted, the woman's more than half-eaten.

3. NO MAN COMES AMISS

THIS leopard was, without an effort, catholic in its tastes, especially when hungry. It seldom ate mere venison, or touched the dogs which common leopards love, but nothing human ever came amiss. It never heeded caste. It ate woodmen. It ate policemen. It ate the village artisans, especially leather workers, caught outside the villages. It ate a holy hermit, and was fond of priests. It ate postmen. It ate pilgrims. The pilgrims crowded into bigger parties on its account, and kindled fires at night, and took turns of watching. More than once the leopard came upon the pilgrim sentry, not very wide-awake, and killed him suddenly. The rest were safe for that night, but did not sleep much. A solitary ploughman in a field, as he turned his cattle at the corner, was seized from behind, and had rest from his toil. It seldom happened that even the bones were found. The leopard did not eat the bones, but there were other beasts of many kinds and sizes to finish what was left.

The total of its "kills" came in the end to about three hundred, more or less, spread over a "considerable time" as these things go, that is to say, a year or two, more than a year, "a good deal more than a year," it was said. In the long-drawn life of a man, who is very long lived for a beast, it can very seldom have happened, if ever it did happen, that any man, with all the helps of mechanism, has killed so many leopards.

4. ITS WAY OF DOING

"HOW could you be sure that this 'kill' was done by this particular leopard, and not by another?" was my frequent question, variously answered, according to circumstances. It had a style of its own, one seemed to feel, after hearing a few of its exploits. There were instances of men hunting it, who were killed instead of killing; but, curiously enough, its most peculiar feat was a failure, from the leopard's point of view.

It went into a big village one day, between four and five o'clock in the afternoon, and in broad daylight strode through three-quarters of it, passing between two rows of houses. Swiftly as it seemed to sweep past, it must have been going slower than usual, for it looked right and left as it went, sending piercing looks into many screaming interiors. Near the farther end it turned and walked straight through the open doorway into an old man's house, without pausing, as if it had come by appointment. The old man was alone inside, and lay dozing. It took him from his bed, and carried him away, and, strangest of all, instead of going to the outside of the village near that end, retraced its steps by the way it had come.

Men's shouts now mingled with piercing screams and the old man's cries for help, and the leopard saw in front of him, blocking his path, nine or ten men with big sticks. "By the grace of God" they had found it in their hearts to face the monster, with no better weapons than these. Give honour where honour is due! There was courage needed for that.

With the dexterity of a Boer commander, who had ambuscaded a detachment but found an unexpected hostile force in his rear, the leopard grasped the situation, and changed his plans. Turning aside and passing between two houses, he escaped unhurt, but dropped the old man, who was also unhurt in body, though badly shaken in nerves.

The long evening hours did not drag so much as usual that night in the village, but by three or four o'clock in the morning there perhaps was nobody living there who had not forgotten his excitement and fallen asleep; and now the hour was at hand when the cocks would waken the world; but there was a ruder awakening than usual that morning there. From the old man's house there rang out piercing yells. In a few minutes every man within hearing had come to it, with whatever weapons were at hand, and as many as could enter crowded in to hear the old man's story.

"I was sound asleep," he said. "I seemed to dream of a rat gnawing something beside me, and, gradually, between asleep and awake, I began to hear a kind of scrape-scrape-scraping. It was so strange that I grew broad awake, trying to make out what it was. Then I knew it was some beast on the mud-roof above me. I lay and lay and listened, and wondered what it could be. It sounded like dogs at first, but I concluded it was something else. No dog could scrape like that. I thought of going outside and looking, but I felt too tired to be bothered. I lay and lay and looked at the inside of the roof, where the scraping was. I did not expect to see anything. I looked there, just because the scraping was there. The place was there, right above my face as I lay on my back. Just as I was taking a kind of last look, before falling asleep altogether, I saw the leopard's two eyes shining at me through a big hole in the roof. There's the hole!" ...

There was indeed a hole, and some of the villagers said that in running up they saw the form of the leopard disappearing in the moonlight, and the roof outside showed marks. "Nightmare," I suggested, but Bingham would not allow that. The marks showed that a leopard had come; and I had to admit that, though there was no direct proof that it was the identical leopard, the odds were about a million to one that it was, if, as the Privy Council Judges have suggested, as a good rule in doubtful cases, we pay regard to the likelihoods arising from known habits and undisputed facts. (I have simplified their verbiage, but that is their meaning.)

5. THE FINAL FIGHT

THE chief evidence that one leopard did all the "kills" credited to this one was the uninterrupted series while it lived, and the cessation, for a while, when it died. But, though practically uninterrupted in time, its killings varied in place, to the perplexity of its pursuers. More than once, when most of those who were seeking it were in one locality, ambuscading half-eaten remains, it went elsewhere, and started afresh, where it had the advantage of being unexpected. It took little pains to remain incognito. It might have travelled far without eating, as other tigers and leopards often do; but this leopard was as self-indulgent as railway passengers now can be, in comfortable expresses, and beguiled the time by eating, as they do. It seldom went a hundred miles without killing somebody for a meal.

Colonel Bingham could not say whether it was helped by the people being deprived of fire-arms; but thought that probably nothing had happened in the Central Provinces to make any difference to the leopard in that respect. A great many guns were given out to likely persons to hunt it, and many young officers, and some no longer young, not military men only, but civilians of all kinds, taking short leave on purpose, when they could not otherwise come near it, gave their leisure to the hunting of this multitudinous murderer. "I never saw such cordial co-operation," said Bingham. "Rival hunting parties forgot their rivalries, and helped each other to the uttermost." The beast was beginning to obsess the minds of men; and, here and there, fields were lying waste, uncultivated, through fear of it.

More than once a man with a gun was killed by it, which does not, however, mean that a leopard can openly "fight" a man with a gun. It means that when a leopard can take a man by surprise, a gun upon his shoulder is no protection. They said so and explained it, to a postman who had succeeded to a vacancy which the leopard had made. Nevertheless the man continued to flagitate his official superiors for a gun, until, wearied by his importunity, they gave him one. Then, as he went his rounds, that postman's inquiries after the leopard had a new significance.

The sight of his gun was pleasant to the villagers, and they praised his public spirit. He deserved their praise. Bethink you of the mails he carried in the broiling sun, as he plodded many weary miles along the dusty roads, and how long you would have volunteered to add a gun and ammunition to such a burden. What made his conduct the more praiseworthy was that he knew the gun would not save him if the leopard were on the war-path and saw him first. In fighting of that kind, as in guerilla war, it is often only the first glimpse that counts. When the rule is to kill at sight, then to see is to conquer.

He had been carrying the gun in this way some weeks, at least, perhaps for months. It had ceased to be needful for him to ask questions as he went from village to village. At sight of him, anyone who had news came to tell it. Many a time he laid his burdens down, to let someone far away but beckoning to him come to where he was, and then they would sit and talk together as if time had barely even a relative existence and did not count for much. Nobody ever grumbled. The rural mails were never in a hurry.

One ever-memorable day he was met outside a village by many of the men who lived there, coming out to meet him, and hastening to relieve him of his business burdens with unusual solicitude, leaving nothing to occupy him but the gun. Then with eager whispers they led him through the village to a big tree on the farther side of it, half bare of leaves. "See the leaves at that corner, high up. He's there, he's there. We saw him go there. Watch till the leaves shake. He cannot move without shaking them."

The postman got ready his gun, probably putting the end of the barrel on a rest, though I am not sure I was told that. It was unfortunate for the leopard that there was no wind. The air must have been rising, as I have seen it under similar conditions, hot from the ground, as from a furnace floor; but even through the shimmering atmosphere the postman could see the leaves were still, fixed, as if made of metal. The leopard waited long, but so did he. And all was hushed. Then he saw a slight, slight movement, just visible among the leaves; and then he fired.

It was some time before the leopard came down, and still longer before anyone ventured close enough to the body to be sure it was dead. But whatever reward had been offered was now payable to the postman. The details of the post-mortem have been sufficiently indicated already; and indeed they were no part of the life of the leopard, which, almost immediately after the postman touched the trigger, ended suddenly. And so does this—its history.

XVIII

ON HEADS IN GENERAL

THE earliest human tools were weapons too, mere sticks and stones; and perhaps the earliest great discovery, before the invention of fire and in days of infinite antiquity, was the importance of heads.

The value of the discovery was due to the natural weakness of our limbs and teeth and nails. The other beasts were better provided with natural weapons and neither needed tools nor made them. The importance of heads did not concern them at all. The lions and tigers, who are regularly killing men and cattle in the way of business, do it as we kill fowls, by a sudden jerk of the neck. They have other ways, but they seem to like that best, as Homer noticed, and we can see to-day. *See* Pope's translation, *Iliad*, v. 206, etc.:

> "... When the lordly lion seeks his food
> Where grazing heifers range the lonely wood,
> He leaps among them with a furious bound,
> Bends their strong necks and tears them to the ground...."

That is exactly the principle of the improved drop of the modern hangman, and swift and painless enough to please the most humane; but it needs a greatly superior force. The hangman is magnificent; but he is not war. Herein lay the importance of the discovery that hitting the head could stun and kill. Thereby the primitive sticks, by which our long-forgotten ancestors straightened their backs and stiffened their feeble knees, became clubs; and men began to face the lions in their path, and other enemies.

But for this great discovery we would have remained as restricted in diet and outlook as the chimpanzees. Whether tending cattle or cultivating the ground, men must be ready and able to take the open field and hold their own against all comers.

Accordingly, we find that the discovery was familiar in the remotest of recorded times. The wearing of helmets is a fashion as ancient as civilisation itself. The Rig-Veda Aryans had helmets, and the Homeric Greeks, and in the ancient classical *Odes* (iv, 2, 4, 5) a Chinese poet, perhaps coeval with Homer, tells of a potentate:

> "He's thirty thousand men afoot,
> Who handsome helmets wear,
> With shells and bright vermilion strings
> That flutter in the air,"

thus anticipating the "red coats" of England. Indeed, that is not the only coincidence of old and new. The Homeric chiefs went among their men, in times of confusion, striking right and left with effective, home-made sceptres of wood, like modern policemen with their truncheons. The helmets of the police make the likeness almost palpable.

In the House of Commons a touching medieval survival is the wearing of hats. It comes down from the days when the steel-cap clapped on the head was the first step in a breach of the peace, and the head uncovered was the silent, unmistakable symbol of the peace-making speech, the soft words to turn away wrath. Little as he thinks of it, the member, who takes off his hat and stands up to speak, is led by a beautiful old custom to assume an attitude such as Themistocles has been admired for expressing, when violence was offered him in council, and he said, "Strike, but hear me." Meanwhile, upon the table lies the unwieldy metal bauble, meant to represent the mace or loaded stick of the Speaker, who presides and makes no speech, but silently tables his tool as if intimating, "My voice keeps order and my club gives law."

Every other mace as well as his, and every sceptre and staff of office, is merely a sophisticated emblem of the original reality, which is a common stick. The weapons of ancient Egyptians and Chaldeans are ancient indeed compared to anything in Europe; but they are modern things, as of yesterday, compared to the cudgel from the woods. And what is perhaps the most remarkable fact of all, while fashions change in war-tackle as in ladies' dresses, the primitive cudgel abides the same; and under primitive conditions it is wielded to-day by the hands of contemporary men, exactly as it was wielded by our forefathers, who preceded history so far that, in our books, we speak of them as "missing." We mean no harm, and we shall, all of us, be missing some day. So there has always appeared to me to be an antiquarian interest in what is certainly, for other reasons too, the best leopard story I know.

In 1886 a Burman farmer was working in his fields, about twenty miles from Thayetmyo, in Lower Burma, and noticed a leopard seize and carry away a calf. He picked up a stick and ran after it, shouting and waving the stick. The leopard saw him and paused and looked at him; but did not drop its prey, as the man had hoped. He fingered the stick in his hands, not taking his eyes off the enemy, and felt, to his joy, that it was a "male bamboo," a bamboo solid inside, a very strong and formidable cudgel, light enough to handle quickly and heavy enough to kill a man or stun an ox.

They continued to eye each other askance, he and the leopard. He would have been happy to see it drop the veal and go. It would have been well content to depart without hurting him. But to go away supperless was not its intention, and to let it take away his calf was not his.

It was interesting to study how they had manoeuvred, the leopard trying to reach cover without approaching the man, and the man to prevent that, without risking an encounter face to face. This lasted long. There was plenty of active patience on both sides; and strategy so admirable that I afterwards regretted that I did not make a plan of the ground and record it all. At length the leopard ventured a bound over a bush and the man came within reach of it sideways, and lifting high his "male bamboo," he dealt his first smashing blow on the skull. Everything turned on that. To fail to stun the leopard would have been most dangerous. But he did not fail. He stunned it; and, with a shower of rapidly-repeated blows, he killed it, and not only saved his veal, but also earned the twenty rupees reward that is always payable for killing a leopard. Surely it never was better earned.

I happened to be in charge of the office of the Deputy Commissioner at Thay-etmyo, when he came for his reward, and held the inquiry myself. I noted the details carefully, because friends in the station, one of them a veteran who had been a quarter of a century in India, had nothing to tell to equal it; and, in the twenty-three years that have passed since then, during which I have heard on the average more than one leopard anecdote a month, I have never been able to verify anything so good as this.

XIX

THE UNFINISHED SPEECH AND DANCE

IN fairness to the eloquent hero of this adventure it should be told, lest any reader does not know it, that wounded leopards are as dangerous as wounded lions or tigers. There was one that was clumsily handled by villagers in Burma a few years ago, and six men died out of those it injured; and I know a man who has told me, with a shudder, that he has twice seen a clever hunter at his side killed by a wounded leopard "charging home."

It was early in 1888, and on the plains near the mouth of the Sittang river in Burma, that I was one of about twenty men with rifles who gathered round a big and leafy tree, in which a mortally-wounded leopard had taken refuge. None could see him; and, when his growl was hushed, we could not even guess his whereabouts. It grew tedious standing there, like waiting for a train that is late. Many men fired at moving twigs, on the chance that he might be below them. "He ought to be in bits by this time," said one at last, "and falling down in detachments." But nothing fell, not even a drop of blood. It became more and more difficult to keep the villagers surging around at a safe distance.

Then out stepped a brave sepoy, and, heedless of the dissuasive shouts of his companions, he prepared to climb the tree. I shouted "stop"; and he grew eloquent, not in the style of Bengal, but in the best Indian manner, heated sincerely by seeing himself balked of a chance of distinction.

"What is the danger to *me*? Am I afraid of anything? Let cannon and rifles thunder and rattle, I will walk into myriads of them if I am bidden. What is a leopard to the like of that?

"I want to *show* what I can do. I will show I cannot be afraid. O, let me go! Do not bid me stop! What is a little leopard? I could take a tiger by the paw!

"It is a duty to slay that leopard, a duty to face and kill him, a duty to the people, a duty to the Sarkar." ...

Here note two things. First, see the innate instinct of obedience, illustrated by the reference to the Sarkar or Government. Fancy any European talking of it in such a connection without derision. Among our very soldiers it would raise a laugh. Well indeed do the Indians say, as they are now doing, that it is Europe that leads and pin-pricks them into anarchy. The other thing to note is the fine oratorical tact of the speaker, worthy of Demosthenes. There was not the faintest allusion to what we all knew, that the leopard was sure to be dead presently. This did not make it less dangerous to close with him, but only made it quite needless. The speech ran on:

"It is a duty to slay that leopard. Through this big village he went ravenous, seeking whom to devour. He terrified the women and children, and made the men shiver, while the sky rang with shrieks. He stalked as a master through the town" (here the orator, by a sweep of one arm, included the adjoining village to the north); "and the country shuddered with horror" (here, with a sweep of both arms, he included the entire countryside).

In fact, the leopard had been in search of a superfluous village dog, and when he found himself noticed and heard the people yelling, he skulked from bush to bush till he was shot, and then ran up a tree. The orator expressed the matter differently. There is a great deal in the way of putting things. What he next said was:

"He left the woods, the home of his kind. He came among the dwellings of men. Shall we make way for him? Shall he be suffered to ravage and run away? Shall he come and go like our master, as if we all were sheep and he the eater? No! give me but the word, and up I go, and take him by the paw, and fling him down. Danger? What do I care for danger? O, let me at him, to show how brave a man can be and make the beasts beware! For, of all the duties a brave man has....

At this moment he looked up, as if at the sky, but saw the leopard, suddenly visible, coming down the tree, and hastily ran back, and was seen and heard no more.

A curious sequel is worth telling. The wounded beast ran into a bush; and a young Burman policeman, who understood of the sepoy's speech only that he was boasting of bravery, resolved to show himself the better man, and sprang forward, dancing a beautiful *pas seul*, and brandishing a big knife, the Burman sword, a handier weapon than ours. "I'll finish the leopard," he cried, and started for its hiding-place, running past me.

It was a pretty sight. We never see now in Europe the solo dances still visible in Burma, and some other eastern countries, on religious high tides. We can only read of them in the Hebrew Bible, which tells of King David casting off the trappings of royalty, and leaping and dancing before the ark in a scanty garment, and so scandalising the genteelest of his wives, Saul's daughter, Michal, who quarrelled with him about it. A dance like David's, if you are lucky, you may yet see in Burma; but hardly again, in this new world of breechloaders and explosive acids, hardly but by some rare accident, can anyone see what we saw then, a spontaneous Pyrrhic dance done singly, so to speak, a man dancing forward, flourishing his sword, to a deadly encounter.

A most deadly encounter it might have been. The leopard was shot through the lungs, and bleeding to death, inwardly. I thought I had noticed him spit blood, and anyone could see he was badly wounded. But he was only dying, not dead. His eyes flashed in the dark below the brushwood, where he lay, and he raised his head and half sat up, showing his teeth and growling, a very loud, monotonous, continuous growl.

I just was in time to knock our hero down, within five yards of the leopard, and step between him and it, quickly joined by one or two others. There was nothing to do but stand ready. The uplifted head was lowered, slowly; the growl grew less, and was punctuated by pauses, which grew longer and longer. There was a long pause, during which there was nothing to hear but men's breathing; then the dread silence was broken by the voice of a young Burman, creeping past me on all fours and crying, "Just let me pull its tail...."

It was an idle day that followed, which gave them leisure to enjoy themselves. About twenty-nine men spent it dividing the corpse. They quarrelled, and I quoted to them the proverb, "The lot causeth contention to cease." Sure enough, it did so. They cast lots in peace, and told me that eating such a beast made men partake the strength and courage of the dead. I thought of many things, as I listened, such as Marco Polo's story of tribes in Southern China, who were so sure of acquiring fine qualities in this way that, if a traveller seemed uncommonly beautiful or otherwise gifted, they sometimes killed and ate him. It is a strange belief, and, in one form or another, it has appeared in many countries. But all the same, whatever I happened to remember on this occasion, the prevailing feeling was that the next time there was such a job to be done, with such a crowd, it would be alike expedient and gracious to—delegate the leadership.

XX

THE BIG PET CAT

ONE evening in the nineties I went to dine at the house of a friend in Burma, and was unexpectedly greeted at the entrance by a leopard almost fully grown. He received me with the same restful manner of dignified armed neutrality that may be seen on the features of a domestic cat, or of an old family servant, observing a strange visitor.

"Do the others know?" I asked the host, meaning the other dinner-guests, not yet arrived.

"Yes, they all know him, but none of them like him, or maybe it is that he does not like them, I don't exactly know what is the matter. He seems to feel by instinct that you're a friend. Dear old fellow!" and the big cat laid its head confidentially on his thigh, and rolled its eyes dubiously in the way cats do, while a fat hand caressed its fine fur tenderly, lovingly.

"It'll be rare fun to see the rest arrive." It was indeed a pleasant entertainment to see that bachelor's house being entered as if a very distinguished hostess were receiving the visitors. The sight of "Mr Spots" made the most free-and-easy a little constrained in manner. They kept their eyes upon him; and as he moved about at his ease, they made way for him with an agility of quick politeness more common in Frenchmen than in Englishmen. But though he engrossed their conversation as much as their thoughts, there was a lack of heartiness in their appreciation which seemed to sadden their host. He tried to keep the fine animal beside himself.

"Pets should always be young and growing creatures," he said, as he scratched its head, and with many mingled puffs and sighs went on to say, "They are a nuisance when they grow up.... You lose their affection, you see.... Women are just the same.... This beautiful beast does not heed me now, and at one time no puppy could be fonder.... He would lie on his back to be tickled by a straw, and play with me by the hour.... He hardly ever snarled, even at the servants. Look at him!" The gentle beast was made to show his teeth and opened a capacious mouth.

"Yes, indeed," said one. "I've done nothing but look at him since I came in, and have had my hand on my pistol already, once."

"He won't hurt you. He's *had* his dinner."

Another visitor sent his dog home, and opportunely remarked that as leopards were fond of eating dogs, they felt at home with humanity as lions or tigers never could. It was hunger only that made these bigger beasts eat men. The normal tiger or lion would run away from a child, or at any rate pass it by. But even a well-fed leopard might take to "long pig," meaning humanity, in simple wantonness, for a change.

"I hope he always has plenty of salt with his food," said one. "Might I tell the boy to fetch some for him now?"

"Why, in all the world?"

"Because it is the salt in human flesh that is said to be the great attraction."

"You don't suppose my leopard spends his time in studying chemistry, do you? I tell you he would not eat you if you offered yourself. His belly's full."

"Mr Spots" yawned and looked round the company with an air of royal indifference. His master continued to scratch his head. In obedience to a gesture, he submitted quietly, when a servant fastened a chain on his neck, and reluctantly but unresistingly he let himself be led away.

"I'm very sorry," said his master, looking after him affectionately, almost as if apologising to the pet. "That's what is hurting his feelings," he explained to us.

"What?"

"The chain—the restriction—the want of confidence is spoiling his fine temper." After a pause he added: "As I was saying, it's the lapse of time. Pets should always be adolescent, and women too."

"Not women," protested one, who quoted "Age cannot whither her nor custom stale her infinite variety."

"It's not variety that *I* want," cried he. "I hate change. I would like my pets never to grow up. It's the change I object to. It's horrid, these transfers...."

"Hillo! Are you transferred?" we cried, more interested than surprised; for, as readers are probably aware, the Europeans of every kind in the east are at the best respectable vagabonds, globe-trotters by trade, and only a few derelicts, who are settling down to die, can have a fixed abode.

"Transferred? No, no—I don't mean that. I was thinking of transfers of affection," he explained, and he proceeded to discuss the claims of various Zoos, and the chance of poor "Mr Spots" being more happy in one than another, like a mother discussing her daughter's suitors.

Amidst the merriment that arose when all constraint was ended, he was advised to wed, and seemed to take the advice most seriously. He did send away the leopard, and did take a wife, not long afterwards; and as he was a good-hearted man, I believe she is a happy woman; but she little suspects who was her predecessor in her husband's affections.

XXI

THE LEOPARD THAT NEEDED A DENTIST

THE excellent American dentist at Madras had me "at discretion" in 1908; and as he worked he began talking, in the kindly way some dentists have, about things in general, and in particular, when encouraged and led to that topic, he spoke about the science of his useful art.

"What spoils the teeth is want of use," said he. "Look at cats! What fine teeth tigers have!"

"When they are young," said I, "are you aware that tigers and leopards often die prematurely of starvation, because their teeth fail them? There is no kind of living creature that needs more than they do the services of a really competent dentist. See!"

He looked over his shoulder with a start, as if half expecting to see some strange customer; but it was only a common messenger....

Resuming his work, he began recalling all he had heard from various patients about cats' teeth; and suddenly ejaculated, "You're right, you're right! I had forgotten what a man told me he saw in the Nilgiris. From a distance, but close enough to see well, he saw a big leopard seize his dog as it played on the road. The dog got loose, in a surprising way. The leopard caught and mouthed him again, and then again; and finally let him go and disappeared as men approached. Three times that dog had been seen in its mouth, and yet there was not a scratch on the body of the dog. The leopard could not have had a tooth in its head."

XXII

THE DEVIL AS A LEOPARD

IN 1891, in Shwegyin (pronounced Shwayjeen), then the headquarters of a district in Burma, but now decayed, because the railway went another road, I became aware as I sat in office of an unusual hush in the precincts of the public buildings. My messenger came uncalled into my room, and stood as if struggling to speak but unable to articulate. My head clerk, the excellent Babu Chowdry, followed him, though it was an uncommon time for him to come in. With obvious difficulty and hesitation, almost stammering, the Babu said, "The devil has come to town."

Ah, if I were only a fictioneer, what a brilliant opening this gives for fine writing. It might be indulged in without fear of contradiction; for, if Babu Chowdry read a thing I wrote as an account of our talk, he would not only affirm it to be true, but honestly believe it. All the King's Counsel in London, cross-examining in partnership, could not shake him, or do anything but make everybody, themselves included, believe him the more. His transparent good faith would convince them. This is not ironical, but the simple truth. If I wrote in the Kipling fashion, keeping faithful to what the Babu could recall, he would trust me for the rest, so that the story might be told in this way.

"The Devil has come to town," said the Babu.

"Show him in."

"But he is not here. He's in the town."

"Send for him then."

"But he won't come. He ..."

"Tell the police to fetch him."

"How? He ..."

"You should know perfectly that no warrant is required. He can be arrested without a warrant if he won't come quietly, were it only for being without a visible and respectable means of subsistence. Send a note to the superintendent."

"But it isn't a man. It's a Devil, and a leopard."

"A leopard?"

"A leopard, but a Devil."

"Shoot it."

"But it's a Devil."

"Shoot it, all the same."

"But it's a Devil, and so the rifles won't go off."

Instead of all which, to tell the downright truth, instead of any invention, I looked in silence awhile at my excited clerk as he repeated, half mechanically, "The Devil has come to town," and guessing that perhaps a tiger, which had been flurrying the place for some weeks, had paid a mid-day visit, I stepped outside to the verandah to see what the matter was, probably telling somebody to go for a rifle. I looked in all directions, but saw no stampeding, such as might be expected if a tiger were strolling anywhere near. There were many marks of general consternation. Everybody seemed to have stopped suddenly whatever he had been doing. The one detail capricious memory supplies is the sight of a man at a refreshment-stall, who had paused with a spoonful of food half-way to his lips, and stood as if petrified as long as I saw him, gaping and listening. Next I noticed the District Superintendent of Police, Mr W. G. Snadden, a sensible, first-rate man, coming from his office, which was in a building adjacent to mine. Without waiting to be asked, he shouted to me, "Don't you bother. It's only a leopard frightening people at my house, and I'll go and see what the row is and come and let you know."

"Anybody hurt?"

"I believe not."

I felt Babu Chowdry watching me to see if I was satisfied. He drew a deep breath. "That'll be all right," we said to each other, and both returned to work. He came into my room a minute later, and said impressively, "The people do say it must be a Devil, as the rifles won't go off." He waited to see the effect of the announcement, but getting only, "That'll be all right," he returned to business.

In an hour or so Snadden reappeared, looking tired with laughing. This was what he had to tell:

"My wife had a fright yesterday. A leopard had been seen prowling round the house. A servant said it came upon the verandah, and stood on its hind legs and looked into the nursery, where the baby was, and also a dog." (Mr Snadden intimated in some way that he had doubted the story.) He continued: "I told my wife it would prefer dog, but naturally she did not wish it to have a choice. So I set her mind at rest by leaving a military policeman with a rifle to hold the fort when I came to office, explaining to him what to do if the leopard returned. It came all right, about the same time as yesterday. They say the cook was in the act of showing the policeman where it issued yesterday from the jungle, when they saw it reappear.

"The man loaded, aimed, and pulled the trigger. The cartridge did not go off. He slipped in another noiselessly, and aimed again. There was no hurry. The leopard did not see him. It was standing still, apparently taking a deliberate view of the house and servants' quarters; looking for a dog, I do believe. No man could want an easier target. After aiming carefully he pulled the trigger, and for the second time the shot did not go off.

"This seems to have flustered him, so that he made an audible click as he put in a third cartridge, and the leopard heard it and looked round and saw him, and turned to go away. He took aim at it. It turned its head round for a parting glance at him just as he pulled the trigger again. For the third time the rifle failed to act. The shot did not go off. The man was left standing, half distracted. He said that as it disappeared the leopard swelled to the size of a tiger, and the glare of its eyes as it looked at him made his heart stand still. It could be no common leopard that bewitched his rifle so.

"Everybody in the house gathered round him to hear his story. That was when my wife sent a man running to me. The policeman half-walked, half-staggered to the lines" (the huts where sepoys lived, near Mr Snadden's house), "and there he was when I went up. They had had a glorious scare. By George, how quickly the panic spread!" reflected Mr Snadden. "They were shivering with funk all round the court before the man, who was running from my house, arrived there. I had noticed something was amiss, and was making inquiries to find out what it was before he came."

"Had the man loitered on the way?"

"No, I think he came straight. The panic round here was not his doing, whatever it was. It came up from the bazaar. I've made sure of that. It seems a miracle. I've been round pacifying the town. The bazaar was upside down, business was stopped, women were shrieking and running after their children a mile away from my house, within a few minutes after the leopard disappeared into the bushes. I cannot understand it."

"Was the beast seen elsewhere?"

"No. The panic was all about what had happened and the rifle not going off."

Neither of us ever knew how the panic spread, though Mr Snadden had a fine scientific curiosity about it, which made him take much trouble inquiring. He concluded his report on this occasion, thus:

"It did not last long at the lines. The man had hardly told his story more than five times when the Subadar (the principal native officer) pushed his way into the middle of the crowd to hear him, and, listening to him, took the rifle out of his hands to examine it. He lifted the hammer, and pointing to the leather on the nipple, asked him, 'Did you remove *that*?' The man looked stupefied, shook his head, and relapsed into silence, and the excitement ended. The men were very good about it, laughing only a little and not unkindly. They did not jeer at the poor fellow, but rather pitied him, for the accidental oversight that had made him look so foolish, and given him such a fright," and made him miss the reward of twenty rupees, more than a month's pay, which he would have got for killing the leopard.

When the truth was known it was easy to pacify the town.

XXIII

THE GALLANT LEOPARD

THE lions and tigers and leopards cannot bring libel suits or arrange duels. So men can call them cowards with impunity, and often do; but it is not fair, and surely all who have been long enough in the woods to know better should do justice to the beasts that are dumb. Besides, there is a real joy in telling the downright truth. It is apt to have the merit of novelty, for one thing. That is why it seems right to tell in 1909 an adventure that befell three gallant officers in Upper Burma, a little more than a dozen years ago.

Three real ornaments of the British army, and one of them so highly placed that in confidential moments after dinner he spoke to me not of his debts, but of his savings and investments, were riding abreast together through a forest. Three finer specimens of "Britishers abroad" the army could not have furnished. They combined all its best qualities—the wild daring of the Irish scallawag, the steadiness of the Englishman, and the cunning of the Jew. If they had all been of one kind, whether scallawags, Englishmen, or Jews, they might have come out of this adventure less perfectly. Great is the advantage of a judicious mixture!

What happened was that a leopard was looking for a meal as they came along. He was not hunting men. He was crouching among the bushes beside the road and watching, as a cat watches sparrows, a crowd of monkeys gambolling among the trees, and unconsciously coming near him. He is at home in the trees, and very fond of monkeys; but they are too nimble for him, if they have a chance. So he was biding his time, till one of them would be within reach of a sudden spring; and none of them had noticed him, when the three officers came riding past.

Now, whatever the attraction was, probably curiosity, what is certain is that the advent of our gallant three caused a sensation in the little world aloft; and, as the miniature men and women of the woods crowded to see the very latest samples of British officers, they saw the leopard too! And with wild hullabaloo they hurried far away.

The leopard was angry. Had he not cause? Who were these men to come and spoil his sport? They, on their noisy iron-shod horses, prancing along, with their orderlies clattering behind them, coming as if the world belonged to them? He felt like another Jonah, who could answer the Lord inquiring, "Doest thou well to be angry?" with a heart-whole emphasis, saying, "I do well!"

So he came boldly upon the road on which they were galloping and stood upon it, facing them. He took no pains to hide himself. He was no longer in the mood for crouching. He waited for them; but he did not lie in wait. His lips were ajar, and every muscle tight—a pretty picture!

"Good God! There's a leopard!" cried the son of Jacob. See how deeply rooted is piety in the Semitic soul! Men have known that man for nearly twenty years, and never heard him mention God at any other time.

They all drew bridle and dismounted. Even the scallawag consented to do that. The Englishman called for his gun. An orderly handed it to him.

"By all that's holy, you're not going to provoke him by peppering him with snipe-shot?"

The Englishman agreed not to fire, as they had no ball-cartridges. But the leopard was not aware of that. The road was along the side of a slope. The ground went steeply up on one side of it; steeply down on the other. So the leopard, "lightly and without apparent effort," like a cat leaping upon a chair, sprang upwards, and sat behind a bush, 15 or 20 feet above the level of the road.

"Slight as the cover for him was, it would have been ample, if we had not seen him go behind it," said one of the men to me afterwards. "We remarked how well he knew to hide himself. Till he went behind that bush we would not have believed it could have covered anything. Once he was there, it was only because we had seen him go that we knew he was there. But for that, we would have seen nothing. The ground being above us was a help to us, and, knowing where to look, we could see the outline of the leopard plainly through the leaves. He had not allowed for that."

No; he had not reckoned on the watchfulness of three men resolute that the *élite* of the British army should not be made into cat's-meat. They held each other back, so to speak, without any difficulty. They could see that where the enemy sat was like a magnificent spring-board. If he had selected the eldest of them, and leapt with his usual accuracy, he and his chosen one would have been a hundred yards down the glen together in a few seconds; and the excitement in army circles would have been very great. Half a dozen men would have "got steps."

But these three were too wary. They—felt their value to the Commonwealth. They *would* not pass in front of him. Nothing would induce them. It was, "You first, sir," for a long time, till the leopard was tired of it, and saw the game was up. He leapt down lightly and crossed the road before their faces, with a deliberate swinging stride, looking round at them as he passed.

"There really seemed to me to be something of a swagger in his walk," said one of the officers, naturally imputing to the leopard the feelings of a man and an officer; but in truth the leopard had no swagger in his mind. He looked at them in passing, as at creatures he had to keep an eye upon; but, far from thinking of impressing them, he was as indifferent to their feelings as the rocks. In Hamlet's phrase, they were less than Hecuba to him. They were merely passing animals, that had disturbed his hunting, and he was now quitting them as he would a herd of deer that had got wind of him and held aloof.

What seemed his swagger was the unconscious dignity of his gait. I have seen it in a tiger, crossing a road in the moonlight, when he thought he was unobserved. Many men have remarked it. It may be seen in the common cat occasionally, and has been explained in various ways. The swift movement by long strides and the silent footfalls are easily noticed; but there is more than that. The dignity of cats is one of Nature's effects, which we can see and admire, but not reproduce. How could we, standing up on our hind legs and to that manner born, ever do more than mimic it? The most puissant of potentates may call himself the son of the sun, the cousin of the moon, and the father or grandfather of all the stars; he may be named in sheepskins and figure in sheeps' heads as the King of kings and Lord of lords, the Emperor of emperors and Czar of czars; but he is first cousin to the monkey all the time. His gold lace and purple cloaks, his tinsel hats and thrones maybe as high as pyramids, cannot make him cease to be funny when he swaggers; and, at the best, you half expect a wink. Nothing can give us the born dignity of the feline fellows. But we need not envy them. Soon, very soon, in a century or, at the latest, a millennium or two, there will be none of them left, except perhaps the household toms and tabbies. "So runs the world away."

Thus it was without any thought about the officers, who were standing abashed, that the leopard moved down the steep slope into the depths of the glen, abandoning all hope of well-fed British beef, and perhaps deciding to try once more for the monkeys.

"Hope springs eternal in a hungry heart."

It is only needful to add that this adventure was told me by one of the three. I have not been able to get leave to give the names; but that does not matter, for the leopard did not know the names himself. It was enough for him, and must be enough for us, to know that they were strong and healthy men, and their orderlies the same; and to the leopard the iron-shod horses may have appeared to be equally formidable. Yet, with just cause of offence and an empty stomach to stimulate him, he faced them all, and departed only because he saw it was useless to wait for them to pass. They *would* not go in front of him. Was ever leopard so honoured before? These men would not have deferred so much to a British lord, much less to an Italian pope or common emperor.

If leopards dealt in art, that would be a scene for a picture; and fain would I have sent the men's photos to an R.A. of my acquaintance; but to ask them for that purpose would have been as hopeless as to ask leave to give their names. So any inspired artist who pictures this scene must paint the officers' faces from his fancy. All that I am permitted to certify is the truth of the adventure.

Bravo, Mr Spots!!!

XXIV

A DUMB APPEAL PUT INTO WORDS

THE Griffin at Temple Bar, a lump of metal like a medieval nightmare, is one of multitudinous monstrosities such as Burns described:

> "Forms like some Bedlam Statuary's dream,
> The crazed creation of misguided whim;
> Forms might be worshipped on the bended knee,
> And still the second dread command be free;
> Their likeness is not found on earth, in air or sea!"

The significance of the Griffin, however, goes deeper than the conventionality, which alone the artists deride; for it is only half an explanation to cry "conventional." What made it "conventional?" Why did men convene to admire such an object?

One has to grope among the beginnings of history to be able to guess; and for that purpose, one has to stoop to the mental level of wild backwoodsmen, not men of civilised breeds who have reverted, like the mustangs of South America, but real, wild backwoodsmen, none of whose ancestors have ever been anything else, since time began.

On trying the thing, I found it as easy to think with them as ever it was to keep down to the level of civilised men, carousing after dinner, when

> "The soul subsides, and wickedly inclines
> To seem but mortal, e'en in sound divines."

Of course it is a commonplace to connect the Griffin with the winged lion of Babylon and other misshapen beasts. But Babylon was as much sophisticated as London is to-day, and as far removed from primitive conditions.

It is among the wild backwoodsmen, if anywhere, that one can reach back to the real antiquity; and if you listen to them at home, especially when they have forgotten you or suppose you asleep, you gradually realise what a great place is filled in their minds by beasts of prey, and in particular by the little-seen-but-much-felt feline foes. Many a man and woman among the jungle folk has never beheld them at all, but few have escaped their depredations. They combine the terrors of force and cunning, and abide a bugbear to humanity, from infancy to age.

Perhaps this may be best illustrated by one of the most famous incidents in the life of Confucius, dated by the *Family Sayings* at B.C. 516, about the time when Darius was sacking Babylon. Here is the paragraph in the old Chinese history

(translated by Legge, *Li Ki*, II. II. 3, 10.)

"As he was passing by the side of the Ta'e mountain, there was a woman weeping and wailing by a grave. Confucius bent forward in his carriage, and after listening to her for some time, sent Tsze-Loo to ask the cause of her grief.

"'You weep, as if you had experienced sorrow upon sorrow,' said Tsze-Loo.

"The woman replied, 'It is so. My husband's father was killed here by a tiger, and my husband also; and now my son has met the same fate.'

"Confucius asked her why she did not remove from the place, and on her answering, 'There is here no oppressive government,' he turned to his disciples, and said, 'My children, remember this, oppressive government is fiercer than a tiger.'"

It takes an effort for a modern man to feel the force of the words of the sage. The tiger means so little to us, and meant so much to the weeping woman and her neighbours. Still harder is it for us to realise the primitive ignorance of the exact shape of the enemy. Even to the few backwoodsmen who have seen one dead, it soon becomes a vague recollection. The infinite terror of the beasts and the ignorance of their forms are not the less indubitable facts, because they are so far beyond our ordinary comprehension; and these are the facts that perhaps explain, so far as we can explain, the grotesque shape of the Griffin. We must remember that our Zoos are a modern invention, almost like firearms; for two or three millenniums do not make antiquity in a world so old as ours. In the days when Griffins first took shape, whatever was the most hideous object would seem to be the best likeness of the horrid reality.

But the Zoos should let us know better now; and our writers and speakers should teach us better than to hate the beasts of prey. It is quite unnecessary. There is something coldly impartial in their war with us. They do not hate us, any more than the rocks do, or the icebergs. Red, "red in tooth and in claw," they remain unconscious instruments of Fate, and serve to stiffen us. If they kill us, it is in self-defence or for food. There is no wanton cruelty; but there is no mercy. There are surprises, but no treachery. Even the French do not feel themselves betrayed, when it is the wolves that win. There is no sentimental humbug about this war; but also, no excuse for ferocity.

I never visit a Zoo and see the poor prisoners behind the bars without hearing, with the mind's ears, a greeting, an appeal for pity, as if the poor big cats were really saying what they can only symbol in silence.

"Look at and pity us! You will not have such cats to look at long. Lions and tigers, leopards and jaguars, the species now all perishing salute ye, O men!

"We are neither grotesque nor hideous, neither wicked nor cowardly, neither cruel nor treacherous. We are merely cats. We had to live in the only way for which we were adapted.

"The war between you and us is nearly over now. It has lasted long, but the end is at hand. The world is lost to us big cats, and we are passing away, on the wings of the wind....

"Woe, woe to the conquered!!!...

"Ye may lay aside your fears! Do lay aside your fears, for fear is cruel. Ye have no need to fear us any more. We are your prisoners of war, and spared to make a human holiday....

"We killed or left alone, and cannot guess why ye do otherwise; but we cannot understand ye at all....

"We look around into daylight that is dimmer than darkness, and see not why we are here. We submit, because we must; and we are dying, dying, dying! All your devices but prolong our deaths! For life needs liberty. There is no life in prison for cats, or for men....

"The species all about to die salute ye!

"Have pity on us, O men!!!"

XXV

THE FOX IN THE SUEZ CANAL

ONE afternoon, about the end of the nineteenth century, a steamer was passing southwards through the Suez Canal, and as I sat in the shade on its deck and looked eastwards over the desert, I saw a little animal with a bushy tail running along the ridge at the canal side, keeping level with the steamer. A slight occasional glance in our direction showed that he knew we were there. At first, he appeared to be a jackal; but, when glasses were turned upon him, we agreed that he was more like the fox indigenous in the deserts and the lands adjacent, the "fennec" as it is called, the "little fox" of Scripture that is said to spoil the vines in one passage. It is a true fox; but smaller in the body and bigger in the eyes and in the ears than other foxes, and more easily tamed. By destroying vermin, he perhaps balances his account with humanity, and is no more considered an enemy than the swallow. He is said to eke out his want of strength by diligence, and often escape his enemies by digging himself into safety. Needless to say, unlike many other foxes, this one digs his own hole, and is never without one, so that it must have been of him that Jesus was thinking, when He said: "The foxes have holes, and the birds of the air have nests; but the Son of Man hath not where to lay His head" (Matt. viii. 20).

A lady, who was watching him with delight, was afterwards sorry that she pointed him out to various idle men. She intended only to give them pleasure; and did not in time bethink her, in what their pleasure lay. Complacent cries of sham excitement were soon followed by—"ping"—a shot from the bridge; and the bright little fox ceased, suddenly, to run abreast of us, fell suddenly lame, and crawled aside.

"Well shot!" cried several raucous voices....

Some Arabs, working near, looked up to see what was being fired at, and leaned on their tools, and spoke to each other, looking, from time to time, at the steamer and in the direction of the fox. In 1886, living at Suez some days, I had had various talks with such men, seeking to sound their sentiments on things in general; and on this occasion, I felt that I knew, as well as if I had heard it, that they were saying to each other—"What bloody brutes!"

What seemed to confirm this guess, was that I did overhear our Indian deck-scrapers making remarks....

Three or four days later, a fellow-passenger was still gloating over the glorious achievement. We were near the south of the Red Sea by this time. Thinking to make him sorry for the wounded beast, I said—"The fox is likely to be dead of starvation and thirst by now."

"Ha, yes," said he, "it isn't likely to live much longer after a Martini bullet has perforated its thigh, ha, ha, ha!"

"People don't shoot foxes in England."

"They kill them in another way. They're just as cruel.... Of course, one would rather have galloped after him; but what can you do from a ship's deck?"

"Not gallop, certainly." I tried another tack. "It is thought wrong, in the Highlands, I have heard, to shoot at the deer, unless you are likely to kill."

"No?" He seemed surprised; but after a pause, he could explain the mystery. "It would spoil the venison," said he.

"Do you think the man who shot the fox in the thigh has nothing to be sorry for?"

"He could not be sure of the head. I think that, on the whole, he did very well. He was in a moving ship, and it was running."

"Are you not sorry for the fox?"

"Not at all."

I was tempted to say I was sorry for him; and could have said so, sincerely. But, after all, he was young, and a human being, though mentally and morally less developed than the Indian seamen or the Arab labourers. I was loath to hurt his feelings. He deserved as much consideration as—the fox. So we changed the subject.

XXVI

SOLIDARITY AMONG THE BRUTES

1. ELEPHANTS

OUR Indian newspapers recently (1909) reproduced reports of a public meeting in London, which had been made remarkable by the presence of the veteran Mr Selous, who had assured inquirers that the elephants do really assist each other in distress. He doubtless gave details of many modern instances; but the newspapers omitted them. So here is one.

Towards the end of 1897, some herds of wild elephants spread far and wide over the harvest fields in Toungoo district, Burma. They had used to do that, not every year, but at intervals, for generations; but this visitation was unusually severe. The area cultivated was greater than ever before, and the villagers had been disarmed. On former occasions the elephants had gone away as soon as the men began to shoot, or even to make a noise like shots, by putting bamboos into fires which they hastily kindled on the edges of the fields; but, on this occasion, the elephants merely paused a little to trumpet to each other, "I'm not hurt," "Nor I," "Nor I." Then they resumed grazing at random, heeding the noises of humanity, the shouting and the rattling of tins and sticks and the bamboo-crackers, no more than the cawing of the crows.

The news seemed to spread in the elephant world that men had ceased to shoot; for as the herd that came first went farther from the hills, seeking pastures new, the farmers who had begun to breathe freely were horrified to see new herds appear. On the morning that the first news came to me, it was followed in a few hours by reports of fresh havoc, like those that rained upon Job. "We'll need an extra officer to measure up the damage for revenue exemptions on that account," was the prudent reminder of a responsible subordinate, expert in reeling off official rigmaroles; but I took an original plan, of which nothing was said, or ever would have been, if that newspaper report had not recalled to mind an incident too good to leave in oblivion. I took the first train to a station that seemed to be the centre of the elephants' operations; and in less than two hours a general engagement was in progress. A long line of men, including military and other policemen and carrying all the firearms of any kind available, advanced as fast as they could towards the elephants, whose demeanour and behaviour could not have been surpassed.

Whenever they discovered that the shots were now followed by bullets, they all ceased grazing, far and near, as far as the eye could reach over a spacious, level plain. They gathered into herds, and, as soon as possible, every herd, with cows and calves on the safe side and fighting males next the enemy to secure the rear, was moving towards the western hills, far quicker than a man could walk. Many of them were wounded, but none were left behind. I had not myself the luck to see, but heard from many others who saw it at the time, a sight that well might be immortalised. A big, wounded tusker had raised the men's hopes. They knew the value of ivory, and hastened to isolate him; but two other big elephants, of which one at least was seen to be a female, ran to him and supported him, one at each side. They held him up as he limped along and joined the herd in safety, and all went off together. The men were left lamenting, and admiring too.

Upon the hills, among primeval woods, the elephants that roam, intent on provender, oblivious of war, resemble the Yankees among the great powers of the world. Their superabundance of material brings water to the teeth of potentates of prey; but the herds of elephants are too terrible to tackle. They graze in peace in the cool glens, and have been known, in thirsty weather, to drink alongside a tiger. Such a thing, at least, has been reported as seen, and often inferred from tracks. Think of what must have been in the heart of the tiger, as he lapped the cool water, with an empty stomach, and eyed the elephants' calves. But "whatsoe'er he thought, he acted right," and departed without hostilities, undoubtedly protesting, in the language of the woods, his love of peace—which was no doubt sincere, under the circumstances.

2. THE BABOONS AND THE LEOPARD

IT is not ill deeds alone that are done because the means to do them are in sight. The same is true of good deeds also. The elephants can help each other better than most quadrupeds, because they have trunks; and so can the monkeys, because they have hands. Herein lay the primitive germ of society. Indeed there is profit in remembering this, for it follows that selfish greed, which is the root of gambling and theft of every kind, is a reversion in the scale of being, not merely to the monkey level, but far below it, to the level of the cats and fishes.

Be the explanation what it may, the mutual helpfulness of monkeys is well ascertained. They could hardly survive in the woods on other terms. A male baboon in Egypt has been seen to turn and face some dogs, and protect and deliver a young baboon in danger of succumbing to them. Here the remarkable thing is that it was the male that did it. Many females would fight for their young. Maternal love is the taproot of life; but the root of society is family solidarity. That the poor "dog-faced" baboon of old Egypt, unaltered for 6000 years, is able to rise so high in the social scale as this, is perhaps what is best worth knowing about him.

The leopard is the great enemy of monkeys of all kinds. This may be said to be true "all the world over," if the American jaguar is called a kind of leopard, as it sometimes is. So it is with special pleasure that one reads of an incident seen in Africa not long ago by Sir J. Percy Fitzpatrick. It occurs in the standard biography of his dog, *Jock of the Bushveld*, pp. 270, 271, 272, and it happened to a leopard that narrowly missed dining upon the hero, "Jock," and so cutting short his distinguished career. Jock's master, apparently, was a-hunting, and saw the leopard pinning a baboon with its left paw in the bottom of a stony glen; but before it could do more, a host of angry baboons descended the rocks towards it, with an uproar that even to a Fitzpatrick seemed deafening; and upon the leopard, which had one paw occupied, they "showered loose earth, stones, and debris of all sorts down with awkward underhand scrapes of their forepaws" (meaning their hands). Nearer and nearer they came, while the leopard vainly threatened them with its free forepaw. Louder and louder grew the uproar. The baboons, like old Cato and the Chinese, believed in shouting and grimacing to frighten the foe; and here they practised that. Neither Cato nor any Chinese warrior could surpass a monkey in twisting the features. The artist who tried to represent their contortions in Sir Percy's book has done his best, but could not succeed. It is "like painting fire," as Carlyle once said.

The leopard became alarmed. It is an Indian proverb that the tigers do not count the sheep; but the baboon is not so negligible. The corpses of a chimpanzee and a lion, it has been reported (but not by Sir Percy), have been found interlocked, the chimpanzee having been disembowelled, and the lion throttled. The leopard could not know that. I confess I have doubts of the truth of the history myself. But the leopard had misgivings as the noisy crowd came nearer and nearer, and let his victim go. Sir Percy watched the triumphant baboons depart. "The crowd scrambled up the slope again," he reports, and he tells us he believed, and so may we, what "all the Kafirs maintained, that they could see the mauled one dragged along by its arms by two others, much as a child might be helped uphill...."

It is a likely guess that the fighting baboons were the adult males of the tribe. This is a guess suggested by another interesting bit of history.

3. THE INDIAN BABOONS AND THE BEAR

DR MURPHY, now civil surgeon at Maubin, in the delta of Burma, where this is written, is a unique phenomenon. That is a clumsy phrase to apply to any fellow-creature, but accurate. He is a perfectly popular European official—popular in spite of being an official, because he is a good doctor, spontaneously sympathetic, kind and helpful, and does not bully or grab.

Two little facts may be told on the authority of the present Deputy Commissioner of Maubin district and his predecessor, to give Dr Murphy the pleasure of seeing himself as others see him, and to give strangers a glimpse of him. In 1908, when he was about to go away on sorely-needed sick leave, the good people of Maubin town, who did not realise how ill he was, got up a petition to the effect that Dr Murphy's leave should be refused, as Maubin town could not possibly dispense with him. When he was expected to return in 1909, the Deputy Commissioner hastened to Rangoon to solicit that Dr Murphy might be posted again to Maubin. That was how he came to be in Maubin this year (1909), when he told me three pretty anecdotes, which, knowing him well, I retell now with as much confidence as if I had seen and heard with my own eyes and ears everything he told me he saw and heard.

In 1883 he and his brother were schoolboys at Mussoorie in the Himalayas; and were in the habit of frequenting a glen where lived a tribe of Indian baboons, "langurs" the people name them. These are "black-faced, white-whiskered, long-tailed, big, grey monkeys, not by any means as tall as a man, but as thick in the arm." They are a different species from the African baboons, but quite as clannish. They live on terms of neutrality with mankind, as the various tribes of men may be said to live with each other; that is to say, open hostilities are strictly avoided on both sides, and stealing is restricted to what can be done in secret. In this instance, as the stealing is all on one side, it might be said they levied tribute upon men, but they do not attack people. School children at Simla have told this writer that the "wild" baboons often sit and watch them, they and the children eyeing each other with equal curiosity.

Of course, they are not Quakers, nor even Hindus. If people flung stones at them, they would fling stones in return. The little brown fisher monkey of Burma, too, will do that. But "in deference to Hindu prejudices," the English leave them alone, so that they have probably never noticed the English. They pay no taxes, these white-whiskered gentlemen; and reciprocate human forbearance. "Live and let live," is their rule with men, and so, in general, schoolboys hardly notice them.

Great therefore was the surprise of the two little Irishmen one day to notice the baboons in a state of excitement, jabbering loudly, and plainly preparing for battle. Their women and children were all huddled in one place, and the big males gathered in another, moving in a body. The boys, as if by instinct, followed the crowd of males "to see the fun," whatever it might be, just as in the Highlands of Scotland, when they were inhabited, the boys used to follow the men at funerals and weddings "to see the fights."

Their curiosity was richly rewarded. The baboons began to bait a solitary, angry bear. The boys were dangerously close to the bear before they saw him; but he did not heed them, which was lucky. A bear, encountered at random, is often "worse than a tiger," it is said; because the tiger can always get out of the way when he wants, but the bear is so slow that he despairs of escaping, and turns and rends the man who has met him. In this case, luckily for the two little Murphys, the bear was preoccupied. The baboons swarmed noisily in the trees around and above him. The elder of the two boys, who alone saw much, said that he saw them incessantly, one hard upon another, come close enough to slap the bear violently with the open palm of the hand on back or belly, on head or side, on whatever point seemed safest of access—Smack! Smack! Smack! Smack! Smack! Their objurgations were like the sound of a cataract. The bear was distracted, snapping and striking here and there, but always missing. The baboons relied on their agility to escape his teeth and paws, with complete success, so far as the boys saw; but the boys did not linger. They had not the feeling of security that the baboons had; and, thankful to have escaped notice, "Run, run," cried the elder, and they ran to a safe distance. There they stood and listened; and when the thunder of the battle and the shouting indicated the bear's retreat, the boys consulted the hillmen, and were told that these battles, which were familiar to the hillmen, always ended in that way.

The glen of the baboons was open to the south and east, sheltered and sunny, and convenient for the fields and gardens, in which the baboons could seek for change of diet. The adjoining glen of the bears had a wetter aspect. True, with all its wetness, it had many oaks whose acorns were dear to the hearts of the bears, and they meant to keep it; but why not have the other glen also? They esteemed the baboons no more than the Belgians esteem the negroes. So, from time to time, an Imperialist bear invaded the land of the baboons; but the hillmen said that they did not think the same bear ever came twice. The reason was that the bear, invading, always came alone. He was too inveterate an individualist to form a Chartered Company. He did not even hunt in couples. So the invader, irresistible as he seemed, was always repulsed by the solid regiment of baboons.

Thus it is that men and baboons are taught the need of solidarity. As Benjamin Franklin quietly and sublimely remarked on 4th July 1776—"We must all hang together, else we shall all hang separately."

4. SIMLA MONKEYS

THE years go by like clouds. In 1902, Dr Murphy was no longer a schoolboy, running about Mussoorie, but a surgeon employed by Simla municipality, and familiar with the little monkeys there, who lived on Jacko Hill. They overran the town, these little men; and took every possible advantage of the toleration of the good Hindus. Perhaps it is needful to mention that Indians are so indulgent that European naturalists in India are continually surprised at the slight fear of men among wild birds and beasts. Thus it was that "Hindu prejudice" protected the monkeys at Simla, though nobody suffered more from them than the Hindus; but even they agreed with Dr Murphy that "something must be done," when the little men from Jacko insisted on entering his house and removing the bread from the breakfast table.

It would be a long story to tell the plans that failed. The plan that worked was beautiful in its simplicity.

Two earthen pots were buried before the eyes of the monkeys, looking on. Only the thick and narrow rims were left above ground. What this was for, no monkey could comprehend, and the more of them that gathered, the more they seemed perplexed. A "multitude of counsellors" may bring confusion instead of wisdom. It was the easiest thing in the world for any of them to put in his hand and feel the emptiness of the pots. But, why were they buried there? "Hum— hum," none of them could tell.

When they were about to disperse and dismiss the matter, as one of the many mysterious eccentricities of men, Dr Murphy put grain into the pots in front of them. This was a sudden illumination to the assembly. To keep grain safe from monkeys is one of the continual problems of Simla life. "And this is *his* way of doing it," thought the monkeys to themselves.

They did not delay to show him what they thought of his device and him. It was really too ridiculous. One of their leading men came straight to the pots and put a hand into one of them, keeping his eyes on Dr Murphy. It was as easy as ever to put a hand in; but, when his clenched fist was full of grain, he could not take it out.

After one or two ineffectual attempts to withdraw his hand, he put the other hand into the other pot, which had been placed convenient for that very purpose. Perhaps, when he put in the second hand, his object was to find out what was holding the first; but when it also touched the grain, the force of habit made him grab with it also, a beautifully human trait of character; and there he stood with both his hands in chancery, meaning by chancery a place that does not readily let anything out that once comes in.

There he remained standing. It never came into his head to open his hands and withdraw them empty. He was an emblem of many an Anglo-Indian, who has "heard the East a-calling," and seeking a "soft job," has wandered where his tribe cannot thrive, but is detained by what he has in hand, and cannot find the heart to forego. The monkey stood there, with both hands full, quite wealthy for a monkey, but a helpless prisoner. If there had been pots enough, his kinsmen would all have come and done likewise; but there were only two, and he had monopolised them; and now he had to endure the multitudinous advice of the empty-handed monkeys, and their criticism, and ...

That was not all he had to endure. Dr Murphy took a whip and proceeded to chastise him, not very severely, but sufficiently to keep him from thinking clearly in the abstract. Then the hubbub thickened round the doctor. The tribe that dwelt on Jacko gathered clamorous. Quick, from the hill and almost every tree, wherever tribesmen were who heard the news, they hastened to the great indignation meeting, all seeming to talk at once, and making hideous grimaces, at which, to their surprise, Dr Murphy laughed aloud. They did not understand his noises and grimaces; but what they could not fail to see was his indifference. Whack, whack, whack! He continued the flogging amidst a chorus of disapproval, quite equal to that of the United Press Association.

The prisoner broke away. The pots had not been very strong; and in his struggles he had broken off the rims. With an earthenware bracelet on each wrist and both hands full of grain, he reached the nearest tree; and there he opened his hands and dropped the grain. "All that a man hath he will give for his life." But in this instance, the general opinion of observers was that the grain was dropped by inadvertence, as the monkey opened his hands in haste to climb, forgetting what he held.

By a similarly inadvertent knock against the tree, he broke one of his bracelets as he went up. Well for him if he had broken both! He joined the crowd that had come to help him, with still a bracelet (of a pot's rim) on one of his wrists. This caused an immediate revulsion of feelings. His friends became his persecutors. They crowded round him, pushing and pulling him, smacking and scratching him, and biting him till the blood came. In a few minutes that leading monkey would have been dead, and perhaps they would have been carrying his corpse to the hill, as some people said they used to do, but suddenly, as the persecuted one was floundering about, the fatal pot's rim broke and fell in pieces to the ground. Behold, he was now as the other monkeys were, different from the rest no more, but sore afflicted and in agony. They succoured him now, like a prodigal returned, and helped him gently away, leaving the kind doctor sad to see how far beyond his intentions the poor fellow had been punished. The doctor declared he would never set that trap again.

But how very human it was! To translate the fine verse of Béranger's song ("Les Fous")—

"As we toe the line, we duffers,
If anyone quits the crowd,
Whatever he does or suffers,
We all of us yell aloud.
The crowd runs to kick him, or slays him,
And afterwards sees it was blind;
Then we set up his statue, and praise him
As a credit to all mankind."

5. CO-OPERATION

WHETHER or not the guess is right that in that hubbub among the monkeys in the Simla trees there was a rudimentary heresy hunt, or, in other words, that the monkeys were screeching whatever in monkey language intimated, "Bad form, bad form," "Order, order," it cannot be surprising to find solidarity such as theirs facilitated, or even made possible, by what can only be called a kind of language. If Max Müller had been beside Dr Murphy one day in 1905 in Simla, and seen what Dr Murphy then saw, he would probably have abandoned the proud claim he has made for humanity to a monopoly of speech. We must be content with the more modest boast of developing it.

The doctor noticed a monkey sitting on the flat roof of a small house in Simla, where lived a man who roasted gram and sold it. The little brown fellow was visibly hankering after the gram exposed for sale on a tray before the door. He leaned over and looked long at the man beside it. Then the doctor saw him go to a short distance and confer with four or five others, two of whom returned with him, and three little heads bent over the roof to study the situation and the unconscious seller of gram.

Then one of them went down the water-pipe behind the house, walked boldly round to the front of it, and openly, before the eyes of the astonished man, took a handful and ran away. The man snatched a stick and chased him; and Dr Murphy noticed with surprise that, of two possible roads, the fugitive took the least convenient for himself, but the one that best kept the man out of sight and reach of his stall. As soon as he was gone, the two remaining monkeys hurried down and helped themselves to handfuls and escaped away, to be presently rejoined by their daring colleague, who had drawn away the man.

It would be difficult to exaggerate the significance of this incident. These monkeys must somehow have been able to speak together and trust each other. To every union of several we may apply what Heraclitus said of every unit,—"Its character is its fate." Solidarity is possible in exact proportion to the degree of honesty prevailing. So the monkeys must have had a rudimentary kind of honesty as well as a rudimentary kind of speech; and that was why they could act on Moltke's maxim—"Erst wägen, dann wagen" ("First ponder, then dare," or, in commoner words, "Think before you act"), and then carry out their plans and co-operate well. We would be absent-minded beggars indeed if we did not see here the germ of that tribal solidarity from which all human civilisation has gradually evolved. Let us never forget our humble beginnings, or despise our poor relations.

XXVII

A RUN FOR LIFE

IN Phayre's *History of Burma* it is mentioned that "the loud, deep-toned cries of the hoolook ape ... resound dismally in those dark forest solitudes, and startle the traveller ..." (ch. xxii). They would startle only those who did not recognise in the resounding "Oo-oo-oos" the voices of harmless, primitive communities of hairy little black men and women, called gibbons, the smallest of the apes that closely resemble humanity. They are probably the strongest of us all in the arms, in proportion to their size; for it is on their agility in the trees that they depend to escape their enemies.

It was in an Upper Burman forest that one of them was noticed a few years ago, pursued by a leopard, which had got between him and the rest of the tribe. What handicapped the little black man — or was it a woman? — was the bareness of the trees. If the trees had been more thickly clad the spotted enemy could not have kept him in sight; but, as it was, whenever the gibbon looked down, the leopard's eyes were on him; and if he paused to rest, it seemed about to mount. "Oo-oo-oo!" On, on, on he had to go, there was no rest for the gibbon. It was like Dante's Hell. He cried pitifully, incessantly, "Oo-oo-oo," and his kinsfolk answered him across the glen; but, what could they do? They could no more mob a leopard than the swallows could. "Oo-oo-oo-oo-oo!"

If he could have rejoined them, however, he would have been safe; for then the leopard could not have tired him out. So said the countrymen, who explained the ways of "Mr Spots"; but in this instance the leopard was able to keep between him and the rest. The intervening space was increasing. Did the little man know some round-about way? "Oo-oo-oo!" The others answered him, as if to say, "Cheer up! Here we are, waiting for you!" "Oo-oo-oo!" His speed increased, as he went farther away, as if he were growing nervous; and surely he had lost his head for a moment when he put foot on the ground, passing a gap, thinking the enemy far enough behind. The leopard was ready for that, and seized him. Then, in that far corner of the glen, there was silence — the silence of death.

XXVIII

MOTHER'S LOVE AMONG THE MONKEYS

IN January 1909 a friend at Pyapon, Burma, told me that, as he was passing through an unfrequented creek near the shore there, between Rangoon and Bassein, the sudden apparition of his steam-launch alarmed a crowd of monkeys. They were on the trees, overhanging the water, and chattering loudly. They hurried away, with leaps and swings, quickly and easily, all but one. He was a *very* little fellow, and there was a big gap in front of him, too big for him; and so he stood shivering, about to fall. His mother saw his plight, and came back and joined him. To take him was impossible. So she sat beside him; and he pressed close to her and clung to her; and she put one arm around him, and, quietly but with quivering lips, she faced the awful apparition, whistling, splashing, puffing. It passed without hurting her or her son. They suffered nothing but the fright.

"Very queer they looked as we came close to them," thought the men on the boat; but their fear was as natural as that of men who see a lion at large. It is likely, too, that that brown mother-monkey had had losses before; and a mother's heart to feel them. Perhaps a memory of old sorrows, dimly present yet, as well as something of the sublime instinct which makes humanity at times self-sacrificing and brave, had strengthened her heart enough to let her face the immeasurable dangers of the noisy, unknown monster.

Instead of laughing at her ignorance, think of our own—how little we can ever know of her or her tribe, how utterly undecipherable, mysterious beyond any hieroglyphics, remain the lines upon her face the "multitudinous wrinkled tragedies" upon the parchment of that little brow! We pass each other close enough; but an infinite gulf divides us, a gulf deeper than that in the parable: for there is no speech across it, no signalling, no telegraphy of any kind. No communication whatever is possible between us, any more than if we lived in different solar systems. Only, we can see and admire in her a mother's love, exactly as we can behold the flashing glories of the kingfisher's feathers, or hear the merry music of the lark. The world is not a nightmare after all.

XXIX

EXIT THE HUNTER

1. UP TO DATE

WHY are there so few heroic tales of our brave boys a-hunting with breech-loaders, may be asked. The truth is that, with modern weapons, hunting is as un-romantic as work in a slaughter-house.

Men may still be wounded by teeth or claws, as I have known one who lost an arm to a tiger, and every now and then a man is killed, although he has modern weapons in his hand; but it is mostly by accident or stupidity, and nearly always by preventable accident, like getting wounded on a railway. It is painful, and may be fatal; but so rare and so preventable that to take the risk needs no more courage than to step into a train.

That is why so many lies are told. The truth is bald. I have witnessed some, and credibly heard of hundreds of hunting adventures, in the most dangerous corners of the world; and read of thousands more. To see the truth, one has to allow for the many events that seem too commonplace to remember, as well as for all the tricks of slippery memory. Statistics are not available, which is helpful in a thing like this; for statistics are misleading, and can be quoted to prove anything. So every man has to generalise from what he knows; and, doing so, I concur in the opinion of those judicious persons who think that the most dangerous kinds of modern hunting are safer in every way than common coal-mining. The percentage of mortality is almost certainly a great deal smaller. Not once, so far as I have been able to believe, not once did any man, with modern weapons in his hands, do anything very heroic, or *need* to do it. The grit was often there; but there was no real opportunity, for it is not the mere taking of risks that makes the hero. The gambling spirit is equal to that. The hero rises above selfishness as far as above fear, and does what he sees to be right, unheeding consequences. In our long war with the beasts, which has lasted so many millenniums, we needed such men at the start, but not now. The brunt of the battle is over, and anyone can finish it.

That is why there is little to tell in our anecdotes of modern adventures, un-less when something happens under primitive conditions. Never did any modern hunter have to face such danger as was faced by a bereaved old Burman grandfa-ther in a village near Rangoon when he took a spear in his hand, and, with other old men, ran after the tiger that was carrying away his grandchild, and closed with it. These old fellows showed a spirit that makes one think better of humanity. But what are we to think of the idle men with breechloaders and servants? What drives them to the field or forest? The heavy burden of life-weariness, the Nemesis of idleness and plethora. The best of them are seeking a relief from real worries, perhaps, and the others killing time, or seeking amusement. Why not? It is nonsense for any man to dictate the pleasures of another; but let us have no cant at any rate, no make-believe heroics, as if the killing of cats needed particular bravery on the part of a man with a battery.

There are few more genuine pleasures in life than that of a European officer, who is at hand to help villagers in India against leopards or tigers, and feels his gun of use; and the wounds, if any, received in that way would leave honourable scars. But such a coincidence of duty and pleasure is rare, and seldom to be got by seeking for it. It is altogether a different thing from the experience of sportsmen in search of sensations.

2. THE LION IN DEATH

HERE is a cutting from a friendly review of a recent book in the *Westminster Gazette* of 5th December 1908.

"Our author, we have said, got no lions. Other game came to him in plenty, but the lions always evaded his gun. Yet he gives us a living picture of a lion hunt, when the harried animal, which has been trying to slink off, at last turns to bay and determines on the fight to a finish:

"'Death is the only possible conclusion.

"'Broken limbs, broken jaws, a body raked from end to end, lungs pierced through and through, entrails torn and protruding—none of these count. It must be death—instant and utter for the lion, or down goes the man, mauled by septic claws and fetid teeth, crushed and crunched, and poisoned afterwards to make doubly sure. Such are the habits of this cowardly and wicked animal.'"

Since Goldsmith described how

> "The dog, to gain his private ends,
> Went mad, and bit the man,"

there has been nothing to equal the humour of this imputed wickedness. A simple person might suppose that the lion paused to spit in poison, or at least deliberately poisoned his teeth and claws; whereas, of course, he merely does not clean them properly. Having to live in the backwoods of Africa, and support himself somehow, he cannot command the toilet requisites of Belgravia. Is not that wicked? And his cowardice, in not standing to be shot at, is uncommonly like that of the Boers. Why should he not avoid the enemy's fire?

In truth, it is plain that the author, as indeed he tells us, was not describing what he saw, but repeating what he was told. His words are not a "living picture," but, if he will allow me to say it, a bloody blur, which no more gives an idea of the real fight than the hospital beds give an idea of a battle. In the supreme hour of conflict, both sides "see red," but not in that way. Neither thinks of wounds. There seems to be no time for that. The only thought is how to kill; and in the glad excitement the manifold details of life and all its conventions, which seem so real in cold blood, are crumpled up like stage properties in a conflagration; and all seems fair in war, and all *is* fair; and the issue lies with the God of battles, and not with the elderly lawyers at The Hague or anywhere else.

So much the worse is it then for the lions, and so much the worse for any man or nation found unready, unprepared. Ah, if we could only regulate battles like law-courts, how different the world would be! But God knows best. It somehow *must* be better as it is.

If this Englishman or any other man would meet the lion on equal terms, as knight met knight in the Middle Ages, I am sure there is not a lion, young or old, in Africa, there is not a tiger in India or Burma, that would not accept the challenge with pleasure. As the challenged party would have the choice of weapons, and a sportsman could not object to fair-play, we may be sure that "Nature's weapons" would be the lion's choice, and the victory swift and certain for the lion, even if it rained Englishmen, to say nothing of other people.

This is an old, old story. Hercules himself had to use a club and poisoned arrows. It is by tools and co-operation that we master the other beasts. The cats are a particularly easy conquest, as they are bigoted individualists. But let us not add insult to injury, and call them cowardly because they dodge us. When next our author is at Lucerne, let him step aside into the garden there and look at Thorwaldsen's lion, cut in the living rock, and see whether it does not lift his thoughts above the shambles. The wounded lion he described, according to the reviewer, was "trying to slink off." Thorwaldsen shows what it was seeking to die in peace. Why chase and torture him more? To get his hide? The lion-hunter, whoever he was, although he risked his life gratuitously, was like a silly child pulling a cat's tail and a thoughtlessly cruel child, for this big cat was in mortal agony.

Machinery-murder, for beasts of every kind, including men, is now a fact inevitable, and, like everything inevitable, it bears a blessing in it, if only we submit to the will of the Almighty, and recognise what He has brought to pass. The blessing latent in this apparent affliction, perhaps, is that we may cease to admire the business of slaughter; and if so, what a stream of blessings may flow from that one.

> "For ever since historian writ,
> And ever since a bard could sing,
> Doth each exalt with all his wit
> The noble art of murdering."

3. KILLING TIGERS AND APES

I HAVE just been invited to invest in an electric apparatus, to be installed upon the tree one sits in, when waiting over a "kill" for the return of the tiger. The difficulty at present is to see to shoot in the dark; and this invention enables you to press a button and flood the place with electric light. If then you are moderately quick, you can shoot the beast while he is blinking at the light, as easily as if it were day. You are as safe in the tree as in a bedroom and very nearly as comfortable on your platform. You can sleep there all night—four nights out of five at the least—

when nothing happens. When the great night comes, that is to say, when the tiger comes, even then you need not lose more sleep than most passengers do in a sleeping carriage on a railway. The swing of the tree in the breeze and the rustling of the leaves make your platform a superlatively soothing bed; and as you lie back and look up at the drifting clouds, and the moon or the stars, you can feel you have the excitements of savage life, combined with all the comforts of Charing Cross; for at your side is a good fellow, willing, for a consideration, to keep watch for the tiger, better than you possibly could, and to watch you, too, and take care that, in waiting, you do not roll over on your back and snore, and finally wake you when it comes. What a dramatic whisper it is in your ear—"Tiger come! Tiger come!" Nothing in any theatre can equal it! Do not be in too big a hurry to fire. There is no need to hurry, if you take care to make no noise at all, and it is well to take time to waken thoroughly, so as to aim your best. If then you fire and kill, you are contented for an hour or two. There might then even be a little danger for you, if you had made a bargain with the Devil like Faust's (see Goethe's text, Scene iv)—

> "If e'er you find me quite content,
> And bidding time stand still,
> To Hell you then can have me sent,
> And bind me as you will!"

But even in that case, the danger would be momentary. "Another" and "another" you would want; and the Devil himself could not provide them—at any rate in Burma, where the many ineffectual days and nights become intolerable, unless you have something else to do as well.

Accordingly it is the Forest officers, whose work is in the woods, who can hunt to most advantage. There was one I knew who killed many scores of tigers, mostly by "sitting up over a kill," in the manner described. I doubt if he knew the exact figure himself. It must have been over a hundred. Besides the tigers, the same man killed perhaps every kind of wild beast in the Burman forests, except only the big ape.

Here, it may be noted, for the information of those who deny the existence of that animal on the Continent, that the writer knew a Mr Bruce, Deputy Conservator of Forests, and a completely credible man, who found his camp-followers attacked by a big ape. To save human life, he shot it, and on laying out the corpse he found it little smaller than the orang-outang. This was in the Upper Chindwin, in the north of Burma; and the villagers, who professed to know it well, called it the "wild man of the woods," which is what orang-outang means in the Malay language.

"I would have done something else," said the man of many trophies to me. "I would not have shot the big ape—at least not within many years past. I once did shoot a monkey in a tree. I used small shot that lacerated its bowels. The poor little beast sat on the bough and held its protruding entrails in its hand and looked at me. I felt as if it was asking me 'Why did you do that?' I swore I'd never kill a monkey again, and never did, and never will."

This reminds one of the common report, which one would like to believe, that a great man of science is occasionally haunted by the ghosts of the apes he has slain. The generous man is prone to remorse. But it is vain. "You can't cure the wounds your arrow has made by merely unbending your bow."

What most needs to be told, however, for it is least suspected, is that with modern weapons and a little skill and nerve, the hunter never has to face much danger. Even accidents are rare, and mostly avoidable. There is little to fear, except monotony and malaria; and green mosquito-nets have long been available for hunters to diminish the malaria. How to diminish the monotony is a problem that remains unsolved.

In India there is less of it—I mean of the monotony. The patchiness of the forests makes the killing of cats more expeditious in India than in Burma. The poor labourers who "beat" have a little involuntary excitement. There is some real danger for them; but for nobody else. The potentates aloft, on elephants or other elevations, waiting to pull triggers, which is their function, are as safe as if they were on the bridge of a battleship, bombarding whales. The ladies could do it equally well; or the ladies' maids. The expense is multiplied a hundred or a thousand times, to increase the amusement; and that is the fashionable Indian tiger-hunting. It differs from ordinary hunting as the Spanish bull-ring differs from the slaughter-house; but, as there is room for thousands to sit in safety round the Spanish circus, and a display of courage and agility by the leading actors, a Spaniard might reasonably argue that his sort of sport was superior in every way. It certainly does supply more fun for the money.

4. THE HAPPY HUNTER

THE happiest huntsman I ever heard of was a fat little Frenchman, who was a guest in a shooting-box in the Highlands of Scotland. His host was some ex-royalty; and one morning the whole crowd were going to stalk the deer, except our hero, who stood watching their departure as cheerily as he could. "Take a gun and potter about yourself near the house," was the parting shout to him; and after a little, finding time begin to drag, he remembered the kindly-meant advice, and shouldered a gun and went off alone.

At dinner-time, he could hardly contain himself till the others had finished telling their doings; and when at last his hints had made them curious, and they asked what sport he had had, he cried: "Ah, my friends, smaller, but better than yours. Just over the top of the first hillock (*petite colline*), on the edge of the moor, I met a glorious herd of Scottish chamois, magnificent wild sheep (*moutons sauvages*), and killed half-a-dozen of them before they escaped. They must have watched you all go to a distance and felt safe. I completely surprised them."

It was only the conventions of sport that made the fat little man ridiculous. The deer were no more wild animals than the sheep. If the deer-stalkers were real hunters, so was he. In danger and in joy, they were the same.

They tell me that this story is well-known in London. That was to be expected. It was too good not to tell. But I heard it in 1894, in the north, from a parish clergyman of superior character, who located it in ground adjacent to his parish. It is impossible that he lied. There is barely one chance in ten that he was misinformed. So, if the "French lord" concerned convinces me that he desires such "immortality" as the mention of his name would give, then his name shall be mentioned, with perhaps a few more particulars. The probabilities seem to me about ten to one that the story is true. After all, a statement is not *necessarily* false, *because* it is known in London.

The pleasure of fighting big cats any brave man can feel. But wherein lies the joy of being what Lord Chesterfield despised, a poulterer? Or of butchering the deer? Why do we not all feel as kind-hearted Plutarch did that, when men are at play, the beasts that help in the fun should have a share of it? Why is there joy in dealing out death? God knows. I have felt it myself; but a man cannot really analyse his feelings. He can only pretend to do that. At times—not always of course, but often enough—our feelings are as mysterious as the stars, which we can watch and photograph, but never explain.

So, when I say God knows, I mean that there doubtless are in Nature, which is another name for the mystery of the Universe, abundant reasons, far beyond my sounding. And I do know a partial explanation, a kind of clue, which our mealy-mouthed manners make me hesitate to mention. Yet, after all, truth needs no fine excuses, and the sentiments of the natural man need no apology. There is a genuine joy in killing. Nobody needs to be ashamed of it, any more than of sneezing. It is born in us all; and to a mind undeveloped, unable to imagine itself in the place of another, cruelty is a pure pleasure, the lively sensations of it not being spoiled by pity. That was how the Inquisitors enjoyed themselves, and executions were always popular. A man likes killing as naturally as he likes sugar. "Clear your minds of cant," as Dr Johnson advised, and it is easy to see in that the true attraction of hunting. How great and genuine a joy it is I never realised till once I watched a lady crunching a praying mantis under a paper-weight, and gloating over its sufferings, just as a cousin of hers, a famous hunter, loved to dwell on his more gory glories. She was sipping a liqueur she liked a minute later, with the same beatific expression of happiness.

The good old salt, Frank Bullen, has lately been lamenting the new and unromantic ways of whaling, when the whales are chased by steamers and the harpoons driven home by gunpowder, and the whales quickly finished by bombs. Indeed, there is no blinking the fact that the fun is out of the business. A man should think himself a fool if he goes on fancying that there is danger or romance, when there is none. The whaler and the hunter, under modern conditions, are as like the old-fashioned whalers and hunters as the saloon passengers in an Atlantic greyhound are like the fellow-voyagers of Columbus or Drake.

5. THE USE OF HUNTING

TO talk of the use of hunting to-day is generally cant, like talking of the danger of it. At the expense of what is wasted in a few years upon foxes in England, it would be possible to exterminate the lions, tigers, leopards, wolves, foxes, jaguars and every other big kind of dangerous wild beasts on the face of the earth; and fewer lives need be lost in the business than went to the building of the Forth

Bridge. The work might be done in a year or two; and in the same time, and still more cheaply—perhaps with a positive profit—the deer and elephants and other wild cattle might all be killed or tamed.

In Great Britain, of course, no planning would be needed. The clearing of the game there shall all be done for fun, "like winking," as soon as the many-headed king, the multitude, decides, if it ever does decide, to end the Game Laws. It is in the Indian and Burman and American and African forests, and in the plateaux of Central Asia, that a little planning and some expense would be required, and a little brave work need to be done. Of course, the present writer is not advocating such a thing. He is fond of cats; and loves wild Nature as well as Nature tamed. But let us have no cant about the business; and recognise what humanity can do in A.D. 1910.

What men go after big cats for is, in general, amusement, just as much as when they go to shoot pigeons; and the one kind of sport is intrinsically, nowadays, no more dangerous than the other. Hunting used to be a school of war; and so was archery. Both arts are equally obsolete for any such purpose. It is only among unwarlike peoples, like the English or the Chinese, that such a thing needs to be mentioned. Officers who go a-hunting are not making themselves better able to lead regiments in battle. It is well if the hunting does not make them worse. There is nothing of military art or science to be learned from sport. Gunpowder and chemicals and machinery have ended that, and made hunting to-day the same kind of thing as golf, or cricket, or any other child's play.

6. IRRESISTIBLE EVOLUTION

I SAW a real hunter a few months ago (1908). He was a Eurasian, in Burma, living from hand to mouth. His clothes were of the roughest, poor fellow, and his appearance showed he had to live very barely. The police said that he was kept alive by his patient mother, who "allowed him to sponge upon her." A passion for hunting had withdrawn him from other occupations. The deer in the woods, along the muddy coast, and the rewards for an occasional leopard or tiger, I was told, enabled him to buy ammunition and a little food. He came before me with his companions, some idle vagabond Burmans of like tastes, because, it was alleged, when other game failed, they had decided to become hunters of men—in plain words, they were robbers. As I unravelled the tangled threads of his history, I saw in it what any man, who has developed healthily, can read in his own conscious-ness, a summary of human evolution from hunting to stealing. From stealing to working is the next step. The hunters shall soon be all vanished from the earth; but the thieves shall be with us yet awhile.

XXX

CHARLIE DARWIN, OR THE LADY-GIBBON

[*Note.*—This study of a gibbon was suggested by the writings of Mr Wallace, the veteran natural philosopher, still alive, who shares with Charles Darwin the honour of proposing the theory of Natural Selection. His writings not being at hand where this is written, his exact words cannot be quoted; but certainly it was because he intimated in some way how much was to be learned by the observation of an adolescent orang-outang, domesticated under natural conditions, that I undertook the upbringing and education of a young gibbon when it was offered to me. The results, for which much of the credit belongs to my wife, seem to justify completely the shrewd anticipations of Wallace.]

1. CHILDREN OF AIR, IN GENERAL

Children of air, without the wings to fly,
Like apes, we mount the trees to reach the sky.

WHY not? Are not our arms better than wings, the implements of an inferior species? A very slight knowledge of anatomy is enough to let one know that nobody can have both wings and arms. The why of that is inscrutable; but the fact is undeniable. The Almighty has written that in the skeletons of all creation.

What fools we are, when we try to improve on the works of God! In His eyes, it is but as yesterday since our parents, with bent backs and feeble knees, came out of the wood, and, "hand in hand, with wandering steps and slow," they stumbled on their humble human way. Fine roads and cars, big houses and convenient clothes we have procured ourselves; but let us not unwisely forget our origin, nor fail to recognise the Mystery of Mysteries, from which we emerged, and into which we shall soon again subside.

There is something so ridiculous in human pride, it is so silly as well as so sinful, that it is profitable to dwell in thought upon the touches of Nature that link us to our humbler kindred, even to those of our monkey cousins, surviving still. Well might Goethe glory, as we know he did, in his discovery of the intermaxillary bone—the little bone which the apes have between the jaws, but which men were always supposed to lack, until the poet and anatomist found it, latent and disused, but visible yet in every son of man.

On this and many other such likenesses, it is needless now to dwell. Encyclopædias are cheap, and the works of Charles Darwin. Rather consider what has been noticed less, and is equally remarkable, the likenesses in feelings, habits and gestures, which depend less upon the bones and muscles than upon the nerves, and upon the spiritual springs, still more impalpable than nerves.

In learning to swim, for example, the first lesson is, do not lift the arms out of the water; for in water or anywhere else, when men are excited, up go their arms. This is not merely a conventional stage gesture. It has become so, because it is a spontaneous movement in real life. Why? Surely, because our arboreal ancestors, whether it was a lion in their way that frightened them or a bull, would take to the trees, and the uplifted arms were the first step to safety. Besides, the little babies in the trees, long, long ago, had to hang on to their mothers by their arms. The whole significance of the gesture lies in its spontaneity. It is by taking thought that we run. We have to learn to walk, no less than to dance; but the baby, newly born, lifts up his little arms, and thinks of what he is doing no more than does an adult in despair, or a drowning man that is sinking in the sea.

Let Aristotle and Confucius say what they will about the best road in the middle, the habits of innumerable ages cannot be unlearned at dictation. In the hour of danger men are apt to revert, and grope for an escape upwards, like the apes, feeling that that must be the right direction—Excelsior. So "to the hills they lift their eyes" and run, when hills are visible and trees are not.

It is not only in the hour of danger that we feel this itching for altitude. It consoled the sailors who had to climb the masts. At least, they sometimes said so, singing with gusto,

> "We jolly sailor-boys are sitting up aloft,
> And the land-lubbers lying down below."

To this day it makes yachtsmen happy—at least, some of them say so, and it is otherwise not easy to understand their preference for cloths stretched on poles to more efficient modern machinery. Be that as it may, it is certainly the itching for altitude that is the inherent part of the pleasure of climbing knotted ropes and poles and slippery mountain-sides, of drifting in balloons like clouds, or whirring madly about like monstrous mechanical partridges with motors in their bellies. For myriads of ages, our noble ancestors looked down upon things in general from the trees, and the taste revives in us readily, and soon feels as natural as winking.

So, if old fashions of decoration last, and a "coat of arms" is needed for some successful sailor in the sky, he could choose no more appropriate emblem than a noble little gibbon. The mighty muscles of an orang-outang or gorilla might put a man to shame, whereas the gibbon is much smaller than ourselves. He is also the nimblest of all us creatures with legs and arms, and in various ways more like us than any of the others. So let the emblem be a gibbon and a man clasping hands, and the legend these plain words of simple truth—

"TWO CHILDREN OF THE AIR."

2. "CHARLIE DARWIN"

IT was "antipathy to Darwin," they told me, which made a reverend missionary, in the last century, exhort some neighbours of ours, some Christian Karens in Burma, to "shoot at sight" the monkeys and little apes that occasionally took a few plantains from their gardens. The loss of fruit could be minimised in other, gentler ways, as their Burman neighbours showed them. The "heathens" were so "benighted" that they spoke of the trifling losses caused by the apes exactly as the poet Burns spoke of the depredations of the little mouse, whose nest his plough destroyed—

> "I doubtna, whiles, but thou may thieve;
> What then? poor beastie, thou maun live! ...
> I'll get a blessing with the lave (what is left),
> And never miss't!"

It is a wonderful coincidence, which I know for a fact, that the Burmese Buddhist gardeners used phrases expressing similarly these identical sentiments.

The Christians were taught to feel differently. So it was lucky for her that it was in a "heathen" garden that the mother of our heroine was trespassing one day in 1892. Running from the sound of the approaching gardener, she escaped with difficulty, and left her girl behind. Poor frightened little mother, what a loss was there! You never knew the fate of your child. You never saw her any more at all.

The gardener carried the captured one in a basket to my wife, who agreed to adopt her, and named her Charlotte, or "Charlie" Darwin. For immediate company of her own size, she had a nice tabby, with whom she became quickly familiar. The little cats in the woods survive by haunting the trees, and doubtless live on terms of neutrality with the monkeys and the apes. The big leopard is the common enemy of both the little cats and the monkeys. When once a suckling leopard, the size of a kitten, was given us, and my wife tried to coax a tabby to be wet nurse, and the cats of the house were all standing round observant of the stranger, the suckling gave a little leopard's growl, and instantly the cats were panic-stricken, and fled to the roof, and stayed there long after the departure of the suckling, till hunger brought them down. The universal welcome these same cats extended to Charlie showed that her tribe was considered friendly. The first thing I remember of her, perhaps, also, her earliest recollection of our house, was her cheerfully dipping her nose in the cats' dish, and sharing their milk.

She never needed a wet nurse, being more than half-grown when we received her. In fact, our neighbour had caught her pulling plantains. Among the common monkeys, the anxious mothers seem to have a rule of thumb to keep their young within reach, by using the tails as French nursemaids use the leading-strings. "The length of your tail, my child—no farther shall you go." But our Charlie was of the human-like species, and no more had a tail than the reader himself. Besides, she was old enough to be out of leading-strings. Mother and daughter had been alike absorbed in the fruit, and in an absent-minded way had let the gardener surprise them. He said he had never even flung a stone at a monkey, and always been content to chase them away. So Charlie Darwin and her mother had doubtless been presuming on his good-nature, as females are apt to do. But the sight of pretty Charlie tempted him, and he knocked her down, with a clod of earth, he said, and made her prisoner unhurt.

She soon grew to her full height, swelling visibly from week to week, almost from day to day, but the full height of her tribe is below army requirements. She was never much above two feet. Next to the size, the chief difference between her and the reader, if the reader is a girl, was that her arms were proportionally longer and stronger, and her legs shorter and weaker. Her Latin name was Hylobates Hooluck; but, as she never went to school, much less to college, it was never used. And nobody spoke of her as a gibbon. Plain "Charlie Darwin" she was always called, and seemed to like it.

She was not proud, though, if she had been, she might have been excused. The brightness of her face made her a centre of attraction. She seemed to dress well; for though she was never insulted with humanly manipulated rags, her beautiful fur appeared to be like a perfectly fitting black satin dress, of Oriental cut, and gave Miss Charlie Darwin the look of a modest lady, at home in a drawing-room. Her sparkling eyes, like moist beads, were surmounted by big white eyebrows. These set off her features so well that one could understand why European ladies, in more leisurely days than ours, took time to mark their faces with beauty spots.

When moving or standing about in the drawing-room, she tottered at times, and would put her hand on anything convenient to support herself, as many an old lady likes to do; and often she would sit down, with a sigh of pleasure. But Charlie did not sit long anywhere. Her restless agility showed her youth. At tea-time, in particular, she was very much alive. She was devoted to fruit; but her natural good manners, some said, her female curiosity, said others, made her sample everything. She neglected the plain bread but, like other young people, had an almost undiscriminating love for cakes. Shortbread was an exception. She was very partial to it; and it was rare fun to give her none and keep it out of easy reach, and watch the result. She sat demurely unconcerned, as a woman can, till she supposed she was unobserved. Then swiftly and softly she ran to where it was, never taking her eyes off the company, as if too interested in what they were saying to think of anything else; and deftly took the shortbread and resumed her seat, as if it were a matter of no consequence.

The only imperfection in her table manners was her way of drinking from a saucer, lapping her tea as the cats lapped milk. In vain my wife showed her a better example. Habits of that kind are easier to learn than to unlearn; and, after all, men also drink in that way at times, under primitive conditions, lapping of the water with the tongue, as a dog lappeth. (See Judges vii, 5.)

3. RUNNING AWAY

NOTHING can really make up to a child for the loss of a mother. True mother's love is like immeasurable space, and gives humanity its first taste of the Infinite. The fishes know it not, and hardly the crocodiles; but, as we move up the scale of being, it comes more and more into evidence. The rage of "a bear that has lost her whelps" is proverbial. I had a friend in the Chitral expedition who told me that they caught the children of an unlucky she-bear; and the bereaved mother, "though she must have been starving among the snows," followed the army for days, and the sentries had to be on the look-out for her. She desisted at length, and probably died there of starvation and despair.

Among our poor cousins, the apes, there is many a mother might put to shame alike the drabs of the slums and the fashionable females of the decadent sets. So it was not strange that Charlie Darwin moped. Though her stomach was well filled, she had lost her mother.

Her mother was not the whole of her loss. She had lost her clan; for these little beings live together, and the germs of human society are visible in their associations "for better or worse." The human soul can no more develop in solitude than a tree can grow in a vacuum; and in the same way little Charlie seemed to feel an aching void. Repeatedly, in the early weeks after she came to us, she would go to sit on one of the trees on the edge of the compound (or yard); and there she would long remain motionless, gazing across the road to the woods from which she had come. At other times, she would go to the other side of the yard, and sit and gaze across the river, at forests on the farther side. "Where can they all be? Oh, where's my mother?" Her hankering for what she had lost for ever was so plain that we were not surprised when she went away to look for them all.

She was absent for several days. Except that she was not in any of the other gardens or adjacent woods, nothing was ever known of her whereabouts. Many pairs of sharp eyes were watching for her in many directions, to earn a good reward; but nobody earned it. She came back herself. Early one morning it was reported that she was in the tree at the door, the tree where she generally ended in returning from a round in the garden. Her custom had been to come to the ground there and walk across the road and run upstairs. But her natural awkwardness after such an absence, and possibly her uncertainty about the reception she might expect, made her stay in the tree this morning. A servant climbed to fetch her down, and she bit him. She descended to within a few yards of the ground to speak to me, though it was only "Oo-oo-oo-oo-oo-oo-oo!" But as soon as she saw my wife coming down the stairs she hurried to meet her. It was really like a child coming home. My wife handed her a plantain, and she at once began to eat. Then holding it in her right hand, and biting at it, she gave her left hand to my wife; and in that way they went upstairs together.

Charlie was too busy eating to say much that forenoon; and, when she did speak, her words were like water spilt upon the ground. "Words," I say; for I do think it likely that her multitudinous intonations, if intelligible to us—that is to say, if we had understood them as her mother could have done—would have had the effect of words. But we could not understand her, at least not well, though my wife, perhaps taking pity upon my curiosity, declared she could gather that Charlie had had a hard time, and travelled a great deal, and got little to eat, and failed to find any of her relations; and that she was minded now to be content with my wife for a mother, and make friends with humanity, and never run away any more. And, certainly, she never did.

4. SETTLING DOWN

THERE is an excellent man in Burma who is said to have lived many years upon nuts; and an acquaintance of his told me he had been led to the discovery that this was the ideal food, by the consideration that nuts must be the staple food of monkeys. I suggested to vary his diet by a regular consumption of ants. Charlie was very fond of them. She would even pause in eating cake to pick up an ant if she saw one. I doubt if she would have done so for a nut. She used to pick up any ant, even the smallest, with finger and thumb with the utmost facility, and put the prize between her fine teeth and crunch it.

My wife had an egg in her hand one day on the veranda when she was talking to Charlie, who was sitting on the veranda rail. With sudden alacrity, Charlie grabbed the egg, and, holding it with both hands, tried to break the shell with her teeth. She failed. It is likely all the eggs she had received from her mother in the woods had thinner shells than those of hens, and so she did not think of using much force. She turned the big egg round and round in her hands with looks of astonishment; and then, in a business-like way, as if she knew there was just one thing to be done, she broke it on the veranda railing on which she was sitting, and guzzled the contents with such gusto that she smeared her face and soiled her dainty fur with the yoke. The next time she received an egg she was supplied with a saucer to break it in; but never disguised her preference for the primitive way of doing she had learned in the woods. So, to make her use the saucer, my wife had herself to break the egg.

The plan of education adopted was in the style of Rabelais. "Do what you like," was the first commandment. Or she might be said to have accepted Goethe's gospel of self-culture, for she "developed" diligently. She never was teased by any kind of collars, chains, or bonds. There was never any restriction upon her, except that of hunger, which tethers us all, and in satisfying her hunger she could do what she liked.

While the house was liberty hall to her, and milk and fruit and rice and cakes and, in short, the necessaries of civilised life were there, the garden was in dry weather preferred, except of course at tea-time, and at night. Of roses and orchids she could have said what the toper said of beer—she may have had too much, but never enough. To be quite candid, she eyed the opening buds as boys eye fruit. She seldom waited till they bloomed fully before she ate them. When such visitors as native ladies had natural flowers in their top decorations, they had to be warned against Charlie's attentions. It was funny to see her grave little face looking up at the lady caressing her, while the long, lithe arm was reached furtively round to the top or back of the lady's head, and the pretty flower there was deftly detached and brought to Charlie's lips, without any pretence of chivalry.

One bad result of liberty, which happily did not take place, was suggested by the sad fate of a common brown monkey in Rangoon. It lived in the garden of a friend of mine, not far from the Scots Church, and was quiet and respectable until it took to drink. Everything was done to reclaim it, and it was on the road to a complete reformation, when it unfortunately discovered, at the top of a toddy-palm near where it lived, a pot into which a good deal of toddy had run. It could not resist the sudden temptation, and drank so much that it fell from the tree and broke its neck. It is well known that baboons are often sots, and the little brown monkeys are at times no better. Great, therefore, was my relief to see that Charlie, after sniffing the wines and spirits in the decanters one day, showed plainly that she did not like the smell. There were toddy-palms near our house too, but nothing ever induced her to try the effect of alcohol. In this matter, the saving clause, it now strikes me, was that there never was alcohol on the table till dinner-time, and by that time she was always asleep. The force of example is very great on these little bits of men and women, a susceptibility of theirs which is one of their most human characteristics. I once heard a man boasting of having seduced a pet monkey into carousing with him, and drinking beer enough to have a headache in the morning, "just like master." Charlie was never so tempted.

Our house was an old-fashioned, comfortable wooden building, all on one floor, and the floor about 10 feet above the ground, with a deep roof made of wooden shingles. When Charlie decided to run away no more she selected as her sleeping-place a part of the eaves with a convenient view of the interior, and yet far enough from the wall to be out of reach of anybody but a monkey or a bird. Unfortunately (for themselves) our pigeons had deserted their own little house and settled where Charlie decided to sleep. It was interesting and easy to watch what happened. Charlie took what room she wanted, and ignored their existence. For some weeks, I think, they lived together peaceably. Then the birds discovered that their new neighbour was fond of pigeons' eggs, and went away, not because they were meek, for pigeons are pugnacious birds, but because they could not defend their nests.

Another gibbon known to me in Burma was less fortunate in his dealings with "our feathered friends." He was so young and inexperienced that he treated crows as Charlie treated the pigeons, and was mobbed by them to such purpose that long afterwards, when he was full-grown and able to go with his mistress to the tennis-court, holding on by her skirts, or hand in hand with her, it was a favourite joke of wicked men to cry, "Caw-caw-caw." Thereat, in ecstasies of alarm, the little man deserted his mistress, and ran and hid himself under the nearest bush. Luckily for Charlie, there were no crows in our yard, only pigeons, whom she could push aside with impunity. They accepted their fate, and the place where they had lived so long knew them no more.

It was curious to see little Charlie, so weak that she trembled at a dog if it came within reach of her, thus exercising the law of the jungle, that might is right, on what was weaker still.

5. TEASING TOM

CHARLIE'S favourite seat was upon the veranda rail. It gave her a wide and beautiful view of the garden and the river and forests, to say nothing of the far-off mountains blue, her native home, for Hylobates Hooluck is by choice a mountaineer. Indoors, without moving more than her head, by merely looking round, she could see the drawing-room, whereof the veranda was an extension, and, through wide doorways never closed, the much more interesting dining-room beyond.

Dr Clark, once famous as Gladstone's physician, is said to have been fond of telling how he watched a little girl sitting in front of a fire, to which a footman brought coals. The man took no notice of her till she coughed violently; and then he looked round, and a few kind words passed.

"Why did you cough?" asked the doctor, when the man had gone.

"To make James look at me," said the candid child; but it is surprising in a man like Clark that he is said to have quoted this as an indication of the *inferiority* of women. If he really did so, it was because he had not thought the matter out, and was confused by words. The difference between men and women is one of kind, not of degree. It is not a difference of less or more, but of sex. A million women could not make one man; but neither could a million men make one women.

Now it is true that a normal little boy, sitting where the girl sat, would not have felt an inclination to attract the attention of a maid, mending the fire; and it is true that normal little girls are continually acting as the doctor saw that little one act. The gentle sex spontaneously craves to be noticed by the other. Why? Surely, because they have been specialised in character no less than in physical form for domestic life; and their essential business ever is to study and humour the men, whose function is to feed and protect them and their children. "He for God only, she for God in him," remains as true as gravitation, even if we fling the Hebrew Bible aside, and give the great Reality some other name.

That this specialisation of sex comes from a far-off date was curiously manifested by our little Charlie. Indeed it was easy to see, and easy to verify by observation in the hills, that "her people" lived under social arrangements like the patriarchal family. Sir Henry Maine, if he had known it, might have reinforced his argument on ancient law from an antiquity manifested by the habits of these small people, compared to which the oldest days of Rome were but as yesterday. So completely womanly was our pet that many of her doings were conundrums to masculine wits. It takes a woman to understand a woman. He was a wiser man than usual who said—"When I say I know women, I mean that I know I don't know them."

Perhaps no man could ever have guessed what Charlie found amiss with our fine tom-cat. "Don't you see? Tom takes no notice of her," it was explained. "He ignores her existence."

Tom's manners were simply perfect Piccadilly. If Charlie had been conventional middle-class English, she would have been humbled. If French or German, she might have been amused or angry, according to circumstances. Being as irrepressibly democratic as the Burmans and Mongolians in general, she was simply puzzled; and in playing at tig or some other game with the other cats, which was a habit of hers, she might often be observed to be watching Tom with a perplexed look, like a kindly teacher "taking stock" of a backward pupil. Tom never looked at her.

One day, as she sat on the veranda rail, she was seen to be intently studying him. He lay motionless, as if asleep, under an easy chair, his tail projecting far. She leapt lightly down to the floor, ran noiselessly along it, as if on tip-toe, and was in the act of reaching forth her hand to the tail, when Tom sprang to attention, and the threatened tail began to swell and sway from side to side in the air. Unabashed, (for indeed I never saw her abashed, only frightened, and on this occasion she was not frightened), she gleefully ran round the chair, chasing the tail, with merry cries of "Oo-oo-oo-oo-oo!"

Tom sulkily turned one way and another, keeping his tail out of reach, and visibly perplexed. Charlie enjoyed the game immensely. It lasted a long time, and then Tom lost patience, and thrust out his paw, with the claws extended.

He could hardly have hoped to touch her. He might as easily have caught a swallow. The claws did not come within five inches of her; but the savage gesture was an outrage to her feelings. She ejaculated what sounded like a squeak, but perhaps should be called a scream; and as he remained callous and far from apologetic, she turned her back upon the clown and resumed her seat upon the rail. Tom, for his part, with a greater air of dignity than usual, if possible, the sacred tail uplifted inviolate, that is to say, untouched, stalked grandly away; but he had not gone two yards before Charlie leapt upon the floor again, as noiseless as a shadow, and swift "as arrow from a bow," she darted after him and seized the end of his tail between her finger and thumb. She seemed to pinch it, and certainly gave it a sharp tug; and then, like magic, when Tom whirled round, she was sitting on the rail again, making faces at him, and audibly chuckling in the intervals of triumphant hooting, "Oo-oo-oo-oo-oo!"

He gazed at her awhile in bewilderment, and moved away.

> "He went like one that had been stunned,
> And is of sense forlorn;
> A sadder and a wiser cat,
> He rose the morrow morn."

6. EVENING AND MORNING

EVER after she returned from seeking her mother, Charlie eyed the woods like a frightened child, and vehemently plumped for civilisation. No wonder! Death is ever at hand for all beings; but in the woods it seems to press upon you. The very tigers have a recurring prospect of death by starvation, a fact which should mitigate our hatred of them, while confirming our hostility. The Lilliputian tribe of gibbons have lively days, quite full of trouble. They are so human, and yet so much weaker than humanity, struggling to save their carcasses from leopards and Christians by sheer agility and co-operation, living from hand to mouth, picking from the bushes what they can, where any bush may hide a mortal enemy.

I had noticed among the hills that one heard nothing of them at nights; and, watching Charlie's ways, I soon saw why. Having found a cozy corner for herself in the eaves, at the expense of the pigeons, she retired to it at dark, as regularly as Shakespeare's ploughman. She, "with a body filled and vacant mind, got her to rest, ... never saw horrid night, the child of Hell, slept in Elysium...."

She detested lamps more than Ruskin did steam-engines. He sometimes went in trains. She would have nothing to do with lamps. She—went to bed. Vain was it to light her roost and offer fruit of the most attractive quality. You could set the cocks a-crowing with your artificial dawn; but Charlie knew too much. She lifted her head, and that was all. She looked at you a second or two, blinking sleepily; and turned to rest again. We are children of the light, the apes and we, no less than children of the air; and Charlie would not quit her sleeping place until the sun relit the world.

Then she rose and came into our room for fruit. In a country near the Equator, like Lower Burma, sunrise and sunset fall between five and seven o'clock all the year round; and Charlie's hours differed little from those of the villagers. So she came in with the dawn and the morning coffee; but, at that early hour, she would take nothing but fruit, perhaps because she was in a hurry to go out of doors. She did not even give us her company while she was eating. Fruit in hand, she toddled out and away.

She always toddled on the floor, like a child, when she went slowly; but her usual gait was a light run, such as they now practise in some Continental armies, as the least fatiguing way for infantry to cover the ground at times, especially going downhill. You bend forward a little (how much, depends on your centre of gravity), and trot, trot, trot, never straightening the legs. I saw the crew of H.M.S. *Devastation* running about in that way, during some manœuvres in the seventies, and heard men talking of it as "a way we have in the navy, keeps the boys awake, we never walk." So I would have claimed the discovery for the British navy, when a foreign doctor claimed to have invented it, if I had not known that both had been forestalled long ago by the little apes.

Necessity had doubtless been the mother of invention for them, as it is so often for us. These little creatures dare not walk in the woods, as men and big apes can do. When on the ground they have to run for their lives, at the top of their speed. Up in the trees they are safe from a tiger, and even from a leopard, as a rule, if they see him. But on the ground there is no beast needs do them reverence. The smallest adult jungle dog could singly kill the sturdiest of gibbons. That was why Charlie had learned from her mother to trot like a man-of-war's man on any flat surface.

When I paid a morning visit to the stable, she often met me there. She had not walked across the compound; but from some high tree had noticed me and come whirling down. I have seen her rub her hand upon the pony's rock-salt, and then put it to her lips and look at me making various inviting sounds, as if to say, "Try this; it's not at all bad." At other times, like a child, she put grain between her teeth and crunched it. I think I have seen her spit it out; but cannot remember seeing her swallow it.

She would accompany me as far as the gate, I on the ground, she up aloft, and rather quicker for the short distance; but she stopped at the edge of the compound, looking timidly at the woods on the farther side of the road, and never venturing beyond the fence.

Towards eight o'clock, I was told, she was generally among the trees near the gate, where she had a view of the roads by which I would return; but it was not a matter of personal affection. Whenever she saw me in the distance, she knew that breakfast would be ready in half an hour, and hastened indoors to look round, having a fine youthful appetite, freshened by exercise. Her business-like, straight return journey was considered so safe a sign that I was in sight that the cook believed her rather than the clock. The explanation was that breakfast was required at an irregular time, between nine and ten, but regularly about half an hour after my return. So Charlie was pronounced "really useful."

7. TABLE MANNERS

WHEN we were at dinner she was always asleep; but, with equal regularity, she was always impatiently awaiting us at the breakfast table.

A chair was set for her, of course, but never used, except as a stepping-stone to the table. It did not suit her size, and we did not have one specially made for her, as the giants did for Gulliver. She so obviously did not want it that it would have been superfluous.

The knives and forks she examined curiously, but without admiration. Like the Asiatics of old, she kept or made her fingers clean enough to eat with, and desired no better implements. I never saw her use a spoon, except to rap on the table.

Sitting upon the table, she faced my wife and watched her, as if she felt, but in a friendly way, as Frederick the Great felt towards the Emperor Joseph, whose portrait he kept in view, saying, "That is the person to keep mine eye upon."

Though clever at imitation, she adhered to her own ways of eating and drinking, and did not imitate ours. This may have been because her habits of that kind were fixed before she came to us; but we thought her way of lapping was like the cat's.

She did not remain seated upon the table, but walked about upon it, like a *petite* Madame Sans-Gêne, or little Miss Free-and-Easy. At first she was circumspect in her movements and did no damage. But familiarity brings carelessness, and carelessness catastrophes. As the Chinese say, too:—

> "Warily you aye should walk,
> Watching not to stumble;
> Men may safe on mountains stalk,
> And on ant-hills tumble."

So the day came when she tripped, and there was a loud smash. Then she whisked herself to the pole of a curtain hanging near. So quick she went that observers could not agree whether she touched the curtain on the way, or mounted with a hop, skip and jump.

Once there, she found that that perch had great natural advantages. It commanded a complete view of the back premises as well as the dining-room, and yet was not many yards from the table. So she always stayed there, for choice, afterwards.

The place visibly pleased her from its elevation. She liked looking down, and disliked looking up. She showed her preference with a naïve candour that left no room for doubt, and has always seemed to me to illustrate and illuminate the laws of Society.

Of course, she was regularly served. Whatever she called for was handed up. And more than once I recollect that we affected to forget her, and did not look at her or heed her. Then down she came, and walked about on the table, helping herself and chattering in our faces, with many a grimace and "Oo-oo-oo," our small, black Madame Sans-Gêne, with the big white eyebrows, the little Miss Free-and-Easy.

8. DOGS

ONCE it happened that Charlie was left in charge of a neighbour, as she was young and we had to go from home; and in the neighbour's house a dog bit her. When next she saw my wife she flung her arms round my wife's neck, and clung to her with sobs and moans, and all the gestures natural to her sex in affliction, and ever afterwards she seemed to feel that dogs were hostile.

I recollect that once our house was filled with visitors, some local tin-god and official attendants, and one of the aforesaid attendants had a bright little terrier at his heels. Poor dog, his master could not silence the irreverent barkings that interrupted even the divinity his master was attending. Cuffs and kicks were useless. Charlie, up aloft, had fixed the terrier with her glittering eye, and "Oo-oo-oo-ed" at him till he was frantic. When he was thrashed into a moment's silence, and she saw she was observed, she nimbly scuttled away among the upper carpentry, only to reappear in a few seconds elsewhere, and catch the dog's eye again, and "Oo-oo-oo" at him afresh; and then the barking recommenced, and the inevitable beating and yelping, which she seemed to enjoy immensely.

9. EQUALITY IS EQUITY

ALTHOUGH she went about on her hind legs, as we do, she did not despise her four-footed acquaintances, and was always intimate with the tabby, to whom she had been introduced on arrival. It was a pretty sight to watch them dip their little heads together into the saucer of milk. They always started fair, but pussy lapped the better. The milk diminished so fast that Charlie could see that her share would be the smaller one at that rate. Then tenderly but irresistibly she put her strong right arm round pussy's neck and pulled her back, out of reach of the saucer. Charlie went on lapping herself, looking round often at the cat, winking vigorously with both eyes, and uttering various friendly vowel sounds. Here, perhaps, it had better be noted, for the information of philologists, that hers was exclusively a vowel language. I never heard her sound a consonant. It would therefore have been difficult to represent it phonetically. The modulations of tones were too delicate for an Aryan ear; but a Chinaman might have been more successful, and my Burmans caught them well. Her meaning could best have been recorded by ideograms, like the oldest of the Chinese or Egyptian hieroglyphs. But there was no use for such a thing. She did not need it, and would not have learned it.

It was probably the accompanying gestures that made pussy understand her. To be pulled back from the saucer, and tightly held out of reach of it, is what may be called an unmistakable hint. Puss acquiesced. When Charlie thought their shares had been equalled she relaxed the embrace, and puss began again; but though she resumed drinking in a polite, deferential way, as if saying, "By your leave, ma'am," puss never abated her speed of lapping, and so had soon to be withdrawn once more. Occasionally this took place as often as three or four times in the emptying of one saucer; and seldom did it fail to happen once. In fact I noticed that at length they used to *begin* operations with Charlie's arm upon pussy's neck, ready for action. Day after day this went on. Puss never struggled. When the milk was thus equally finished they parted friends. The great rule of equity law, that "Equality is equity," was never better practised; and so profoundly is it in accordance with the nature of things that even a cat can understand it, when constrained.

10. WHERE CIVILISATION BEGAN

BUT where had Charlie learned that "Equality is equity," a rule that has been found beyond the grasp of a "common"-minded chancellor? Surely, in the family circle. Her whole character, and, in particular, the readiness to imitate, upon which I do not dwell only because everybody knows that kind of thing, was that of one who had inherited family instincts, whose ancestors had lived in families for immemorial generations. The habits of living species are slowly modified in the lapse of millenniums; and we were not teaching Charlie tricks, but letting her develop naturally, and observing her.

The mention of imitation reminds me that Charlie could handle my wife's hand-mirror as well as any lady; but the first sight of it raised hopes that were disappointed. She was seen to be moving it back and forward with one hand, while with the other she was groping behind it, until at last she was satisfied that there was no other gibbon there. The great life-sorrow of Charlie was that she never saw another like herself again. It was pathetic to see her looking in the mirror, and then at other inmates of the house, as if asking herself, "Why am I so different?" She was like Robinson Crusoe, without a chance of deliverance; or she might be compared to Gulliver among the giants. Though in proportion not so small as he was, she was too small to feel at home or among equals; and for animals as for men to be weak is to be miserable, and strength and weakness are largely matters of comparison. We petted her so that she did not feel that much; and though nothing could supply the lack of kindred beings, the lapse of time benumbed the pain, and she was consoled.

> "Reader, if thou an oft-told tale wilt trust,
> Thou'lt gladly do and suffer what thou must."

One of the best-known bits of English literature is the sentence which keeps the memory of old Hobbes green, his fancy picture of a state of Nature. —

"No arts, no letters, no society, and which is worst of all" (especially for philosophers), "continual fear and danger of violent death, and the life of man solitary, poor, nasty, brutish, and short."

The great mistake in this nightmare description is the supposition that men were ever solitary by natural habits. Never, never, O Hobbes, since men began to be, never but in artificial conglomerations defying the laws of Nature, and dying in consequence, never did men and women stand alone. Individualism in its extreme form is actual insanity. In moderate forms it has always been common. It fills our jails to-day. It is almost universal among the cat tribes; but wherever and whenever it spreads among men it leads to death. The most primitive of human creatures ever known to maintain themselves have been found to live in families. The human apes, nay, the very baboons do likewise. So it is contrary to science or sifted common-sense to think of our arboreal ancestors as solitaries.

What probably misled Hobbes was the remark of Tacitus, in his *Germany* (XVI), that the Germans, who may have seemed to Hobbes, as to a great French historian, "the last arrived of the barbarians," lived "scattered and apart, just as a spring, a meadow, or a wood has attracted them." But Tacitus goes on to tell how they lived in villages, and were united in tribes or clans, just like the people of Afghanistan both then and now, or the Highland clans till the eighteenth century.

What misled Hobbes is matter of conjecture. That he was mistaken is certain. It would be contrary to all analogies based on our existing knowledge, that is to say, it would be sheer hallucination to imagine that, between our cousins the human apes, and primitive humanity, who both live in families, there was a different kind of creatures in human form, who lived like cats, each for himself, and every man against everybody else. Hobbes, himself, if he were alive to-day, would laugh at that, and in the light of new knowledge he would be the first to allow that, though life in a state of Nature has its drawbacks, solitude was never one of them. Civilisation is the art of living together; and it commenced with family life in immemorial antiquity, before we left the trees, so that it may be said to be older than humanity itself.

11. FILIAL FEELING

IT is a common remark of Japanese philosophers, applying Western science to their Eastern histories, that filial affection is unknown to the beasts, and the last feeling to develop in spiritual evolution, and consequently the first to deteriorate. That is how they have been known to explain the moral inferiority of Western civilisation; for, as lawyers, on legal-political questions, do always—of course in a perfectly honourable manner—adapt their legal principles to their politics, so do philosophers, unconsciously, shape theories to suit their national prejudices. Why not? A man whose trade is words can find reasons for anything; but a man who cares for nothing but the truth soon learns not to theorise beyond his knowledge.

However, I never quarrel with anybody, least of all with the philosophers. They can either stretch their theory, or else say Charlie was not a beast. One or other of these two things they must do, when they know how she convinced her sceptical master that she loved as a dutiful child and was utterly devoted to the lady who had received and fed and protected her—master's wife. A little girl who risks her life for her stepmother is sure to be well furnished by nature with filial piety.

Many were the experiments made to test this, as soon as time enough had elapsed to let filial affection germinate in Charlie, if the germ of it were in her. My wife had long been sure of it, but I was doubting yet, when an indisputable experiment settled the question in Charlie's favour, and so, perhaps, gave her a place in history.

By the happiest of inspirations, one morning, my wife began crying and sobbing while Charlie was still within hearing, at the other end of the house but not yet outside the eaves. "Pretend to slap me," she said, "and make a noise."

I obeyed, and Charlie heard. Swift as a flash, she reappeared on the partition wall, between the bedroom and the dressing-room, and moving restlessly upon it, with arms now and then uplifted in distress, she "Oo-oo-oo-ed" at the top of her voice, and made hideous grimaces at me, and uttered guttural grunts we had never heard before, quite German or Pathan in accent, noises that seemed to emanate from the deepest depths of her being.

By the help of a mirror, I could see her without directly looking at her. Finding threats and expostulations unheeded, she took a leap of more than two yards, and landed on the curtain poles of the bed. I could not then pretend not to see her; but, to her horror, I heeded her no more than before. Then she made another big leap, and landed on my shoulders, and, as I felt before I felt her feet, clapped a hand upon each eye. If it had been serious fighting, as she believed it was, she might have had my eyes out before I was aware of her movement—so quick was she, "like a needle." At least, she could have blinded me for the moment—at the probable cost of her life. She had, in fact, in her desperation, for my wife's sake, ventured to try the identical feat that Ulysses practised on the cannibal monster Polyphemus, whom he blinded in his cave. If one reflects that she could hardly have weighed a stone, and the man she attacked was rather above than below the average of men in size and weight, one cannot refuse to her the praise that properly belongs to a Jack-the-Giant-Killer or tricky Ulysses.

That she was generally timid, as was natural for her size and sex, merely clenches the argument about her filial feeling. Say, if you like, that it was excitement, half-hysterical, that did it. What caused the excitement but her devotion?

Luckily for myself, I had been watching her closely. My hands were on her little wrists in a moment, and no harm was done; and my wife's caresses soon composed her.

I would gladly have repeated the experiment oftener than was allowed, which was only after long intervals about twice; and on every such occasion, the whole drama was rehearsed, the small spontaneous performer never failing to make her death-defying leap. And every time she did it, she was rewarded not with tit-bits only, but with what children dearly love, a pleasant sight. My wife thrashed me. Then Charlie laughed. She rolled from side to side, as she sat on the partition wall, as if "unable to contain herself." She "Oo-oo-oo-ed" approval, and danced for joy.

12. AGREEABLE SENSATIONS

IN the eighth book of his autobiography (*Dichtung*, etc.), Goethe moralises that "with the infinite idiosyncrasy of human nature on the one side, and the infinite variety in the modes of life and pleasure on the other, it is a wonder that the human race has not worn itself out long ago." He explains the mystery by a toughness which, it is now safe to say, must have been inherited from our arboreal ancestors, for Charlie had it in full measure.

The fact was that, when she grew up, she suffered from *ennui*, and no wonder! She had food without seeking it, and was safe from the continual dangers that kept her lively and busy in the woods. Without a husband "to make her uneasy," as the old song says, and no children to work for, she was in the same painful quandary as so many good maiden ladies I know, whose "only labour is to kill the time, and labour dire it is, and weary woe." Often enough it is not their fault, as it was not Charlie's.

> "Full many a gem of purest ray serene,
> The dark, unfathomed caves of ocean bear;
> Full many a flower is born to blush unseen,
> And waste its sweetness on the desert air."

To do her justice, Charlie set to work to amuse herself, unhasting, unresting, in a way worthy of Goethe's disciple, and not only found agreeable sensations for herself, but provided them for her admirers.

As a child of Nature, she tolerated drawing-room monotonies chiefly for the sake of cake and shortbread; but she dearly loved to see men coming to call, especially if, as generally happened, they wore high headgear. Our house had much open woodwork aloft, which suited her as if it had been designed for her convenience. After very little practice she was able to send flying far the hat or turban of any man coming up the front stairs. It added to the joke that they had been duly warned against her. She would show herself and move away when looked at—the shy, innocent creature—but it was only to another beam, where she was unobserved, whence she could stoop upon the passer-by, and with a dexterous touch uncover him. The variety of expressions on the faces of the men, as they looked up at the sweet little cherub who was grinning aloft, was perhaps as amusing to her as to anybody else.

There was a proud Mohammedan who swore his turban should escape, and, flinging dignity to the winds, desirous at any cost of scoring over those whose headgears had descended, he kept his hand on his. So Charlie's usual side-blow merely shook it. The man cried out triumphant—too soon. With the quickness of thought Charlie changed her tactics. Instead of repeating the ineffectual side-stroke, she caught the turban in the middle and pulled it up. The man whirled round indignant, and she dropped it at his feet with a grin. He told her she was a heathen. She answered, "Oo-oo-oo!"

To drop things from a height seemed a perennial pleasure to her. That is a characteristic of many monkeys, and, in many forms, is visible in men and women. To keep to monkeys, I recollect a playmate in the seventies who wept with laughing as he told me how his pet monkey, being driven in spite of his protests out of the drawing-room, had taken refuge, poor exile, in the kitchen. My friend was not allowed to go into exile with him, and was bidden hold his tongue when he called attention to alarming noises. The monkey was meanwhile sitting on the highest shelf in the kitchen, solacing his solitude by pitching the best china of the household upon the brick floor.

Among the most agreeable of the sensations which Charlie was addicted to seeking was that of sliding in a sitting posture—the "sitting glissade" they call it in the Alps. She had no snows, but contented herself with the boards, upon the ridges and dips in our shingle roof. From the highest apex of the roof to near the eaves she came sliding down, pretty quick, partly by force of gravity, partly by pushing herself with her hands. Her hands clattered and rattled on the shingle roof with a great noise, which added to her joy. Once down to near the eaves, she would stop and run to the top again, with looks and cries like those of boys sliding on the ice.

It is surely needless to multiply references to show how human this sponta-neous performance was. As the Cimbrians came down the valley of the Adige, about a hundred years before Christ, the Romans saw with amazement the barbar-ians, "almost naked among the ice," says the historian, as if reporting an eye-wit-ness, sit upon their shields and slide down the Alpine slopes. There is no detail of these old wars that sticks better in the memory than this, and one is reminded of it by our new fashions of adult sliding, so wonderfully like the sport of the brave invading savages, two thousand years ago.

As for her love of noise, nobody can call for proof of the humanity of that. It is self-evident.

Even if the idealists are right who claim that the only cure for *ennui*, and the only way to peace of heart and mind, is the "love of God," or the "love of beauty," or the "love of knowledge and wisdom," or "art," which is not always trumpery, or "music," which is not always noise, or whatever other name we give to the har-mony and the visions vouchsafed to the pure and good and wise, not even the ide-alists, indeed they least of all, can claim to be different in kind from little Charlie. The difference is only in degree. In her humble way, like an inquisitive child, she was for ever investigating things, stroking a tiger's skin, for example, comparing it with other materials on the floor, turning back the cat's outer ear and gazing into it like a surgeon; touching, tasting, handling, whatever was within her reach; for ever on the outlook for anything fresh, like the idle Athenians, who crowded round the first preacher of salvation, in search of something new. This universal craving of mankind is a natural inheritance from busy forefathers who lived aloft, and had to be continually on the look-out. And as Charlie sometimes sat and dreamily gazed upon the world in general, with a puzzled look, and beheld with mingled joy and bewilderment the glorious sun, she seemed to me to be better qualified than any sophisticated Athenian to pay real homage to the "Unknown God."

13. CORROBORATING ARISTOTLE & CO.

WONDERING, if not worshipping, as she blinked at the morning sun, Charlie

Darwin then and all the rest of the day was continually giving opportunities of observation such as would have rejoiced the heart of Wallace. The gibbons in a Zoo are more out of their element than men in a jail. They are surrounded by strange sights and sounds, and stupefied and quasi-paralysed by lack of occupation. We can learn little more from them living there than from their little bodies when they are dead. Nor are pets more satisfactory. At any rate all others I have seen, but Charlie, were too sophisticated. You could no more learn from them their native life, than you could learn the ways of English children in the country by watching poor little guttersnipes, who have never been out of town.

But Charlie was the real wild maid of the woods, the genuine gibbon, unadulterated. She never needed to conform to our ways unless she saw fit to do so, to please herself. It was live and let live, on both sides. She was at home in every sense. Cousins of hers, perhaps actual brothers and sisters, or her bereaved mother, were roving free, not very far away—as free as any wild beast ever is, that is to say, living from hand to mouth as usual, seeking provender. And after all, that is how Nature first made man—

> "Ere the base laws of servitude began,
> When wild in woods the noble savage ran."

One day as I was listening to mingled sounds from across the river, thinking I heard the "Oo-oo-oos" of the gibbons, mingled with dogs' barking and human cries, there seemed to be a look of recognition on Charlie's face, and she also listened; but neither then nor at any time did she make a second attempt to join her relatives, so that her master began to hope that, perhaps, when she was older, some likely bachelor of their clan might be attracted to civilisation by her. It was quite certain she would never revert. She had had her fill of barbarism.

The melancholy moping of her first few days, when she used to eye the woods, never returned after it went away. From dawn to dusk, her mercurial activity never ceased, and that fact seemed to her master to illuminate one of the most interesting problems in mental evolution.

It is not yet very long since Sandow and others have taught us that the best way to develop the muscles is to use them frequently in gentle exercises, avoiding great spasmodic efforts, which strain and weaken them. The same law applies to the mind. There was a Latin jingle to that effect current long ago in schools, which is worth preserving as a bit of old-fashioned wisdom. I never saw it in print, but was taught it orally many years ago by one who had learned it in the same way sixty years before.

> "Gutta cavat lapidem
> Non vi, sed sæpe cadendo;
> Sic vir fit doctus
> Non vi, sed sæpe legendo."

The meaning is this—

> A man's made learned by reading oft,
> And not by rush and shock;

> Just as the water, falling down,
> Drip-dripping, wears the rock.

Assuming for the sake of brevity that the reader agrees to this, which is a matter about which men of sense are generally agreed, what has to be told is that Charlie Darwin, our Charlie, illustrating evolution without studying it, unconsciously suggested that the approved method of steady and gentle exertion was merely a continuation of Nature's way upwards, the identical way that Nature took to bring the apes above the other beasts, and then improve the apes. Their hands provided a ready means of action for many purposes, and their habits of diet, which made them ever ready to eat, provided a perpetual supply of motive power. The great progressive movement, so begun, has never stopped. The restlessness and the *ennui* which cause so many crimes and follies are Nature's impulse, misused or neglected. It comes from habits older than the hills. It is the vital force of each. With it, we may do evil, if we will; but we can do nothing at all without it. The cats can gorge themselves and sleep in happiness and health; but Nature has made that impossible for gibbons and for men.

Of course the only novelty here is the suggestion that continual employment was Nature's way of stimulating the growth of the brain. The doctrine that beings, with such brains as men and apes have now, can find content and peace in healthy occupation, and in no other way, is a very old discovery; but, as there are many to whom philosophy is folly written large, it may make the truth more credible to them to mention that Charlie's habits proved this beyond a doubt, and so corroborated the profoundest conclusion of Aristotle (*Ethics*).

She also ratified the rhetoric of John Ruskin. His declamations against the excessive division of labour were the derision of practical people in the nineteenth century. "Polishing the pins with men's souls! Bah!" With shrugs and sneers they intimated that he was a lunatic. If he had not been rich, he might have been jailed as an incendiary. Rich or poor, he would have been in danger anywhere but in free and happy England. And now England's patience is rewarded by the discovery that Ruskin was essentially right. If our brains have been developed by our innate readiness to "turn our hands to anything," then, assuredly, to restrict activity to one or two mechanical movements is to reverse the natural process, and so torture the mind worse than the constraining bandages torture the feet of Chinese ladies. The damage done to vital organs in that way cannot be compensated by any wages.

Thus were the conclusions of Aristotle and the rhetoric of Ruskin reinforced by the example of Charlie Darwin.

14. THE LAST CHAPTER

BY May 1893, when Charlie had been about a year in her master's house, he had been about two and a half years in the same station, in charge of the same district, doing the same kind of work. The average for the province was a few months. So he should not have been surprised that he was then, on the shortest possible notice, transferred from where he was, in the Sittang valley, in the east of Burma, to a district with headquarters on Ramri Island, off the western coast.

What to do with Charlie in such a hurry, with such a destination, would have been a troublesome question if she had not by that time become independent and able to support herself. It was not that any gibbon-Romeo had found her out. That happy fate had been impossible in the time allowed. If, indeed, we had continued to dwell there in the woods for another year or so, it was the confident expectation of the neighbouring gardeners that some enterprising young gibbon would have recognised her charms, and appreciated the combined advantages of freedom and plenty. An official post, with abundance to eat and drink and nothing to do, truly it was the very kind of soft job that Mr Kipling's heroes roam the world to find. Yes, assuredly, the gardeners were right. We would have had another civilised gibbon very soon. Already somebody was considering on what terms, as to housing and settlements, the managers of the Rangoon Zoo might obtain the family. But, like many another spinster, Charlie lost her chance through no fault of her own. We could not stay, and when suddenly the time came to go, Charlie was ready. She had won her independence differently.

It came about in this way. Our house was on the edge of the town. There was nothing beyond it but some Buddhist temples and the rifle-range. The way to both these places of resort was the road by the side of which, among the trees, Charlie finished her morning exercises, and sat watching for my return, impatient for breakfast. So she was soon noticed by the people, policemen, volunteers or villagers, who were often passing about that very time, and they never failed to stop and watch her. Monkeys are not uncommon; but a gibbon is a rare and popular sight on the plains of Burma. Few of the passers-by had ever seen so human a beast before, not even the Hindu policemen, who hold monkeys in special honour.

Of all the tribes who have both arms and legs, including ourselves, the gibbons appear to be, proportionately, the strongest in the arms. Those of Malaysia, in particular, called "agile" by naturalists, are among the record leapers of the world, clearing at a fling a space beyond the capacity of perhaps any other being without wings. Darwin and Wallace would explain this by pointing out that they are the prey of animals that lie in wait to catch them as they pass from tree to tree, so that those of them who touched the ground the least would be the most likely to survive. The same tendencies are visible in Burma, and though Charlie's immediate kindred are not such record-makers as her cousins in Malaysia, they are fine performers, and so was she.

By slow degrees, not all at once, the little acrobat in black velvet tights became aware of the friendly attention of the observing crowds. It was a visible addition to the pleasure of both sides to be conscious of each other. The people began to applaud. When they saw her enjoy their applause, they applauded the more. She seemed so like a prima donna or actress, that I have never, since then, made the common mistake of supposing the "little airs" of a woman on a public scene to be affectation. Once, in particular, I was watching her unobserved, when she seemed, in her excitement, to have forgotten for the moment breakfast and everything else. She was apparently resting when first I caught sight of her, and she did not see me. At any rate, she was sitting with her back to the audience, looking over her shoulder at intervals to make sure that they were still waiting. Then she began to go bounding round the tree. After a little of this, she went in a corkscrew direction upwards, and when high up flung herself to a neighbouring tree. The feat was received with a burst of applause, in the midst of which she went whirling round and came to the top of the tree, and sat there, on the airiest pinnacle, surveying the admiring crowd with complacency.

This happened oftener and oftener. When I was transferred, all sorts of people offered to take her. So, first, she went to see how she liked the surroundings of the house of the Sergeant-Instructor of the Volunteers. Her subsequent history was reported thus.—

The Sergeant's house adjoined the barracks of the Hindu (Sikh) policemen, who had been the most appreciative of her many admirers; and Charlie was not a chained monkey, but a free woman, though a Lilliputian. It soon appeared that she now needed more admiration than any one man could give. She took less and less notice of the Sergeant and his wife, and stayed more and more in the trees beside the barracks, and at last it was agreed that she was to be common property, while all were there together, but that the Hindus were to take her when they marched away. And that was how Charlie became a camp-follower and the pet of a battalion.

We next heard of her in 1897, when a native officer called upon us at Toungoo, expressly to give us news of her. She was then with her battalion in Rangoon, and as popular as ever. The details he gave have slipped from memory, all but one, which he repeated in English, addressing my wife: "Karlie" (so they pronounced her name) "Karlie is now very fat."

In later years I tried to find out more, but failed. These little people do not live long. There was a rumour that she died in 1905; and, doubtless, she did die, her body returning to dust and air, and her perplexed spirit, as her Hindu friends, and indeed her old master too, would agree to say, subsiding into the great ocean of being that floods the world.

> Like foam that from the sea comes white,
> So come all living things to light;
> Like foam returning to the sea,
> So, having been, they cease to be.

XXXI

THE BRIEF BIOGRAPHY OF A LITTLE BEAR

1. EARLY DAYS

IT was in 1899 and in Upper Burma that two little bears were brought, by villagers who had caught them, to an officer still flourishing as a magistrate in Burma, but averse to fame for himself, though willing that his pets should have their place in history. "They were at first no bigger than that," he said, as he held his hands about a foot apart, "and I took a fancy to them and decided to bring up both."

It was as interesting as if they had been babies, and easier. Indeed the bear has a certain primeval claim upon us, having perhaps been humanity's oldest acquaintance. It is not a mere accident that the Greeks made him a king of the woods and sacred to Diana, and the Red Indians of America made elaborate respectful speeches to excuse themselves for eating him, as if it were a kind of cannibalism. It can hardly be doubted that men and bears became friends at first in much the same way as men become friendly among themselves at college and elsewhere, because they chanced to be neighbours and of similar habits. Nuts were nuts to bears and men, and fruits and eggs were appreciated by both alike. For thousands of years our arboreal ancestors and the bears must have hobnobbed together, both finding it awkward to have to be at home upon the trees and yet move about upon the ground. Ah! how we both did envy the birds! We have risen a great deal in the world since then, and the bears have been stationary, but we need not be proud. While we watch the clumsy gait of the bear as he brings his forelegs to the ground, if he has far to go, and hobbles along, not very nimbly perhaps, but better than we could go on all fours, his very clumsiness should give us food for thought. As he is now, so once were we, that is to say, our ancestors, meaning our arboreal ancestors, not long ago, that is to say, probably less than a million years ago.

When he is young and only learning to walk, his toes being turned in so as to suit his arboreal movements, the bear trips on his own paws and at times rolls over in a ludicrous way, as if turning an unwilling somersault. After such a collapse, his next impulse naturally is to move backwards, as the safer way. But then, his eyes being set in his head like our own, he soon finds that the universe is too complex to allow indefinite blind retrogression; and so he tries again, and makes another cautious step or two forward, with a continuous effort to avoid tripping on his own toes. At last, though not without many a sad catastrophe, he does learn to go forward and follow his nose like other people. This is natural history, an account of how a little bear learns to walk, and it is not an allegory of the Russian empire, as readers might suppose. That was how these two little ones learned, while growing in size and in favour with man and woman. They were in their native climate, and too young as yet to see any difference between humanity and themselves.

It was pleasant to watch them and share their feelings, and escape for a moment from the narrow limitations of humanity.—

> At home in the world, wheresoever I be,
> There's nothing alive that is foreign to me.

I have another friend, who has also been foster-father to bears, and who is fond of illustrating the distinction between instinct and reason by their infantile habits. However small the cub, he never needs to be taught how to bend and arrange the twigs, so as to give himself a convenient resting-place upon a branch. That, I am told, is instinct; and so, I suppose, is licking his paws, which comes as easy as breathing. But once two baby bears were attracted by the smell of honey to a wild bees' nest up a tree. The bees came out with angry buzz and stings. The assailants were young, and had neither bee-hats nor aprons, and they retired, discomfited. Their kind master gave them, as consolation prize, some spoonfuls of honey on a plate. They licked it all up, and then looked at each other with surprise and animation, as men do who are realising something strange, as if saying to each other, and each to himself, "So that was the meaning of the smell we went to investigate."

When the "brutality of instinct," as the French call it, was thus reinforced by knowledge, they did not hesitate. "They did not pause to parley or dissemble." Straight back to the tree they went, and up it, swiftly, steadily, right to the nest of the bees, and tore it open, heedless of the stings, brushing the bees aside as carelessly as if they were flies. They guzzled the honey, and came down slowly, licking their lips, only when it was finished. Surely their foster-father might well be proud of bears like these, and say that they could draw inferences as well as an undergraduate.

In case any reader is led by this history to bring up a cub, let him remember to leave plenty of water in his tub in the bathroom. It is sure to be much appreciated in the hot weather. There is no prettier sight than a little bear enjoying himself in that way, with his two little hands—I mean forepaws—hanging over different sides of the tub, as he leans back. It should, however, be remembered that, not being equal to the use of towels, he likes to go to a bed and roll himself on the bedding when he comes out of the water. So unless there is someone standing by, there should be a waterproof sheet over any accessible bed.

These things are common to adolescent bears. The uniformity of Nature is an old discovery, and one of them is like another. As this is not a treatise on Natural History but a biography of an individual, I must restrict myself to what was peculiar to our heroine and her companion, and leave others to dilate upon what may be generally seen in her fellow-creatures of the same species.

2. UP THE CHIMNEY

IN writing as in living, it is easier to see what is right than to do it. The biographers of Europe would agree that their proper concern was only what was characteristic of their heroes, and not the details of human life in general. "In the abstract," they would all agree to this; yet which of them does it? The difficulty is to discover what is distinctive.

If that is hard for a man who is writing about a man, it is still harder for the historian of a bear. If I were a bear, I would not have been puzzled to know whether the great adventure in the chimney was a thing to tell, or only what any bears would have done. Not being a bear, the writer could not ask his inner consciousness. He had to ask his friends who had bred bears; and when he found that our heroine's master was the only one of them all who had a house with a chimney, the problem had to be abandoned as insoluble. So he has decided, like a certain great author, to take the risk of being tedious rather than elliptical.

The open-brick fireplace with a chimney was for heating, not for cooking; and stood in the hall, near the front door. "I could never discover why it was there," said the unfortunate tenant of the house. The building was an achievement of the Public Works Department, which is surrounded by mysteries and has ways past finding out in Burma.

That fireplace and chimney perplexed the two little bears as well as their master; and once, when there was no fire, they sat down together on the hearth, and meditated; and as they meditated they lifted up their eyes and saw the sky! How their hearts did burn within them, as they gazed upon that light in darkness; and their instinctive propensity to climb made them get up on their hind legs and gape at each other, and rub their eyes and look up again. Like the juvenile hero of Longfellow, they felt the impulse of "Excelsior!" Up they started, to reach that sky. At first, they were quite composed—it seemed little harder than going upstairs; and there was no hurry or flurry. They helped each other. But a chimney that grows narrower as you go up is disconcerting to the aspiring climber without hands. It disturbs the centre of gravity in an unusual way. They fell back, first one and then the other, and again, and again, and again; and ever, like the spider whose persistence cheered the Bruce, they tried again, and again, and again; and still they fell. They became individualistic, but not all at once desperate. There was a sublime fixity upon their countenances, significant of the primeval elemental forces which impelled them, yet nevertheless pathetically human. After all, they were "seeking the light," be it remembered, honestly "seeking the light." Their blind impulsiveness made them all the better symbols of humanity. Think of the European scholastics in the Middle Ages. What were *they* doing for many centuries but trying to climb to the sky through a sooty chimney?

Smile if you will and must, but do not laugh. You would have had no heart for laughing if you had seen the agonies of the bears when strength failed them, and their falls and bruises were—enough! They flung themselves upon the ashes of the hearth in a despair that was equal to that of any man. From nose to tail they covered themselves with ashes—to say nothing of the soot already there.

However, as Byron sings, and psalmists and fakirs have experienced, "the heart may break, yet brokenly live on." When they had had enough of the ashes and the soot, they emerged; and naturally, desiring above all things to be clean again, they rubbed themselves upon the freshly painted walls and nice clean furniture; and when the servants ran to remonstrate, they made for the bedrooms, amidst a general alleluia!

I abstained from asking their master what he said when he came home; and he seemed to appreciate my forbearance.

3. AT A RAILWAY STATION

THE next remarkable incident was on a railway journey, on the way to Ye-U. The guard had charge of them, and kept them in their basket in his own van, where he "could have an eye upon them." This would have been enough if they had been common wild bears, newly caught; but these were civilised animals, and while the guard kept an eye upon them, they kept two pairs of eyes on the guard.

It was a single line of railway, and there were long pauses at every station, during which the guard was on the platform. In one of these intervals, the bears made a united effort, "with a pull, and a push, and a push altogether," and then the shrieks of a stampeding crowd drew the eyes of the guard and the station-master and everybody else to the unusual sight of two fine young bears enjoying a walk on the station platform.

The panic was not unreasonable. If they had been wild young things, their own terror would have made them dangerous. Fear is the cause of cruelty, as Sir Charles Elliot (*Odysseus*) has aptly remarked, in explaining the reciprocal atrocities of Greeks and Turks. But the bright little bears of this history had never known fear, secluded as they were in a happy home. They only wanted to stretch their legs, as other passengers were doing. When that was seen, the shrieks of terror turned to shrieks of laughter; and people made reverent way for them, and followed them with admiring looks, crowding respectfully, without pressing close upon them, as if they had been royalties or popular idols. The railway officials were not teased by any more impatient questions as to when that train would start. It must have been more than a quarter of an hour after the starting signals had been given, before anyone thought of showing the bears and their admirers the need of resuming their places and continuing the journey.

The rest of the life of the bigger of the two, the leader in this adventure, was short, and like the records of common humanity, where "to be born and die, of rich and poor makes all the history." He was wandering about with his chain loose, in his master's garden, and went up a tree. The chain became entangled round his neck; and, when next he was seen, it was the dead body of a half-grown bear that was hanging from the end of his chain. Nobody saw how it happened; but there the beast was—dead!

4. A BREAKFAST AT YE-U

"LIFE belongs to the living," say the wise. Whoever survives, must be prepared for changes; and there is no misfortune so great that a person of sense cannot draw some benefit from it. That is true at times of bears, as well as of men. For the surviving bear in this instance, the sad death of her companion was not without a pleasant result. She was delivered from her chain, and rejoiced in her liberty, like a suffragette. That is why the story of her life is interesting—and short. Incidentally, it might be a lesson and a warning to her sister-mortals in petticoats and running loose; but, to be perfectly candid, that is not why it is written. I do not wish to claim any merit, undeserved. I tell her story just because I liked it.

It is often a pleasure to remember sorrows past, as Æneas reminded his ship-wrecked companions, by way of comforting them. But it may be doubted whether our heroine ever took much pleasure in the recollection of the breakfast at Ye-U.

Three officers came to breakfast with her master; and her usual place at table being filled, she moved about, like a privileged child at a party, suspecting no harm and intending none to any living creature, when one of the men at table gave her the end of a cigarette. She ate it. Whatever else she scrutinised, she had always eaten without hesitation whatever was offered by the hand of man. So she swallowed the end of the cigarette, and became very unhappy.

There may have been moral as well as physical nausea. Who can read what passes in the brain of a bear? Or feel what is in her heart? She may have felt, in a dumb, instinctive way, what Schiller has articulated—

"Oh, she *deserves* to find herself deceived,
Who seeks a heart in the unthinking man!"

She went and lay near the wall of the dining-room, with unconscious dignity averting her eyes from the merry party, and making them laugh by her look of patient helplessness, as she rubbed her stomach with her two forepaws.

A pony was the next performer that morning. The dining-room was on the level of the ground, and the pony, running loose, came to the table as usual for a tit-bit. "Send the beast away," was the impatient wish of a guest—let us hope he was the hero of the cigarette. The host, who might otherwise have gradually given some bits of fruit, handed the happy quadruped a whole pineapple, and bade him go away, intending thus to please his guest and yet not disappoint his pony. Pineapples are cheap in Burma. They are likewise very juicy and good. The lucky pet, who also had the easy confidence of a privileged person, began to roll the big pineapple in his mouth, and was in no haste to depart.

The mischief-maker, if it was he, as we hope, made a gesture to quicken him; and the obedient animal in turning raised his nose above the head of the impatient man; and then there flowed down upon the man a torrent of mingled froth and pineapple juice, all churned together into a sticky milk. He howled, and tried to dodge it, but was unlucky in his movements. The only result was that he received the torrent in two directions. While one stream ran down his face, and anointed whatever took the place of a beard, the other ran down the back of his head and neck, even to the uttermost skirts of his garments.

Then the bear was forgotten; and the other men began to laugh at the man who sat under the pony. They laughed the more when he lost his temper. Even the host did laugh; and let us, who can congratulate ourselves that we have never been guilty of such a breach of courtesy, be candid enough to consider—did we ever encounter such temptation?

What enhanced the fun, and his affliction, was that instead of frankly facing the situation and going to a bathroom, he tried to clean himself at table. After exhausting the resources of civilisation in the shape of handkerchiefs and napkins and finger-bowls, he used towels—big bathroom towels; and still he found purification as difficult as ever did Macbeth.—

> "Will all great Neptune's ocean wash this blood
> Clean from my hand? No, this my hand will rather
> The multitudinous seas incarnadine,
> Making the green one red."

But it was not a troubled conscience that dimmed his eyes. His bodily eyes saw perfectly. The trouble was the real adhesiveness of the mixture saturating his garments and his skin. The language of Macbeth, too, was refined in comparison to his; for, as he glared at the laughers around him, he said ... what I would not repeat, not even in an affidavit.

Our heroine said nothing. *She* did not join in the laughing. She was generally fond of fun; but on this particular occasion, she seemed to be completely self-absorbed, as sufferers are apt to be. There are times when one craves to be alone. She turned her face to the wall and her back to the company.

5. THE BEAR AND THE PERAMBULATOR

HER master loved her as dearly as ever any man loved a dog; and so, when he was transferred from the north of Upper to the south of Lower Burma, he took her with him. This was lucky for her. She had made a bad impression on the man who came to relieve him, although, as himself a father of children, he might have been expected to appreciate her. It was all a misunderstanding.

The new man had come in advance of his family, but brought with him a perambulator, nicely upholstered; and when the gentleman went upstairs to bed, and the servants to their quarters, our heroine naturally proceeded to examine the perambulator, which was exactly the right size for her. There was nobody else in the house whom it suited at all. How could she know, without being told, of the impending arrival of another little thing? Everything thereabouts had been at her disposal hitherto. How could she suspect that this might not be?

Of course she was too young to understand distinctions of property; but, even if she had had a mature human intellect, she might easily have made the mistake she apparently did.

At any rate, what is certain is that, next morning, the fine leather was torn to tatters, and the horse-hair spread about, while she contemplated the work of her paws with complacency. The new magistrate was as unable to express his feelings as our heroine to explain her thoughts. They gaped at each other, I believe. Presumably, she had found the stuffing hot, and wished to make her new toy suit the climate and her taste. But she could not explain all that; and the new magistrate said....

Suffice it for the purpose of this history that he made no objection when her own dear, original master declared that he would take her with him wherever he went. So they departed together.

P.S. — While the biographer of the bear is correcting the proofs of this book at Toungoo, Burma, in June, 1910, he meets the owner of the perambulator, who not only confirms what is here recorded, but even becomes bitter again against the bear, and, warming at the recollection, rhapsodies in his wrath. — "She was a wicked beast. She tore out the insides of my pillows, too. She was eternally meddling. She went everywhere. Nothing was sacred to her at all. I never was gladder to see any pet begone." "But did not N. love her?" it was asked, naming her owner. "O yes, he did, he thought nothing too good for her." What a happy little bear!

6. LIFE IN A COUNTRY TOWN

THEIR destination was Kyauktan, a Burman name that means a "ridge of rock." As you go up the river to Rangoon a low ridge is visible, inland, on the right, almost parallel to the muddy bank, and not very far from it. It is a ridge of rock; but, in that benignant land, there seems to be something indecent, or at least savouring of skeletons, in bare rocks like those of more desolate countries; and in this instance, as usual there, you may know the rock is below, but you see only the elevated greenery. Towards the seaward end of the ridge is Kyauktan, a little country town on a tidal creek, invisible from the ocean steamers. There was the new home of our happy heroine. There she lived in her master's house, amid abundance infinite to her, because she could not measure it. Milk and rice she tolerated, as other children do; but even of these she took only what she wanted; and she had an embarrassing choice of riches of other kinds, enough to make any honey-bear quite happy.

The deep black of her fine fur was relieved by beautiful white lines on her bosom, meeting in the middle, like a necklace with a pendant on the breast. As she squatted on her haunches her nose was little above the edge of the table; but when she stood up to help herself, as she was continually doing, the natural decoration on her bosom was conspicuous, and she almost seemed as if quite nicely dressed.

Table manners she had none. How could she have manners when she had no hands? The word "manners" comes from the word for hand (main, manus). Manners mean a dexterity that hands make possible for men and monkeys, but not for bears. If they had had the hands and we their paws, the evolution of species would have taken a different turn, and the course of the world's history changed indeed! Our heroine had to adapt herself, and did it with great dexterity, but she could not grow hands. Her method at table was to reach forth both her paws, and scoop in towards herself whatever she wanted; and then she would lift things to her lips with both paws, using her nails almost as the Chinese do their chopsticks. It was not her fault that she had to break glasses and upset dishes and make many a mess.

Her master could deny her nothing. It was therefore lucky for him that her tastes were not expensive. She liked fruits best, and the fresh kinds too, which are cheap, not the tinned things. But she was not bigoted. Her appetite was eclectic. Sweet jam was appreciated, and honey in a high degree; but she did not altogether refuse marmalade if she saw nothing better.

Occasionally she was utterly unreasonable, and became troublesome, not by pulling the tablecloth, as did another Burman bear of my acquaintance, but by a peculiarity equally characteristic of a pet that was spoiled. Or it might be attributed to her temperament. It consisted in being so absorbed in what she saw that she forgot everything else, just like the ordinary doctrinaire or idealist or athlete or any other kind of common person, able to see only one thing at a time. For example, if she saw plantains on the table, and wanted them, but did not then want any of the milk or sugar or other things intervening, she ignored what she did not want, and leaned over far enough to include the plantains in her magnificent embrace, and pulled the plantains to her, unheeding all the rest.

No man is perfect. Her master has confessed that he once or twice was so provoked at such a performance as to give her a tap on the nose, whereupon she went and "sulked in a corner," as he expressed it; but how could he tell what she was thinking?

Some said she whimpered for her mother on such occasions. The Burmans say, "When the child trips, it cries for its mother"; but it is not certain that she remembered her early days, for she was but a young thing when she was caught and taken to a man's house. Her master may well have been an indifferent substitute for an indulgent parent; but he was all she had, and his jam was very good.

He was not allowed to monopolise her young affections. She had not been long in Kyauktan before she had explored the town and even found her way to the bazaar or market, where the stall-holders, male and female, welcomed her with open arms.

To tell Europeans of a bear running about loose and being welcomed with open arms in the markets may seem a fairy tale; and though in a narrative of fact it is permissible to tell what is stranger than fiction, still it may be as well to explain a few things that Europeans cannot easily know. The Kyauktan bazaar was a *retail* market, where people were never in a hurry, quite different from Covent Garden; and the bears of Burma have different habits from those of Europe. They are smaller too; but that is the least of the difference.

In Europe, if we mean to be rude and impute rudeness, we call a man a bear. To torture bears was a familiar sport, not long ago—bear-baiting. We still use the word; and big bears ignominiously led captive may still be seen, bemocked to make a foolish holiday. All this implies a hostile attitude which is never seen in Burma.

Perhaps a grim passage in Gibbon's *History* may be quoted to show the contrast. It is in chapter xxv, and concerns the great Emperor Valentinian (A.D. 364–375). He had put his brother Valens on the throne at Constantinople, and taken charge of the rowdier end of the world himself.

"In the government of his household, or of his empire, slight, or even imaginary offences, a hasty word, a casual omission, an involuntary delay, were chastised by a sentence of immediate death. The expressions which issued the most readily from the mouth of the emperor of the West were, 'Strike off his head'; 'Burn him alive'; 'Let him be beaten with clubs till he expires'; and his most favoured ministers soon understood that, by a rash attempt to dispute or suspend the execution of his sanguinary commands, they might involve themselves in the guilt and punishment of disobedience. The repeated gratification of this savage justice hardened the mind of Valentinian against pity and remorse; and the sallies of passion were confirmed by the habits of cruelty. He could behold with calm satisfaction the convulsive agonies of torture and death: he reserved his friendship for those faithful servants whose temper was the most congenial to his own. The merit of Maximin, who had slaughtered the noblest families of Rome, was rewarded with the royal approbation and the prefecture of Gaul. Two fierce and enormous bears, distinguished by the appellations of *Innocence* and Mica Aurea, could alone deserve to share the favour of Maximin. The cages of those trusty guards were always placed near the bedchamber of Valentinian, who frequently amused his eyes with the grateful spectacle of seeing them tear and devour the bleeding limbs of the malefactors who were abandoned to their rage. Their diet and exercises were carefully inspected by the Roman emperor; and, when *Innocence* had earned her discharge by a long course of meritorious service, the faithful animal was again restored to the freedom of her native woods."

Unlike those occidental savages, the heroine of our history, if asked to eat the flesh of men or even butchers' meat, would have felt as much insulted as Bernard Shaw himself. I do not mean that either she or "the Shaw" would rather starve than nibble a chicken; but that their tastes were delicate, and they preferred cereals and vegetables and fruits and sweets to any kind of carcasses.

The Burmans call the bear "wetwun," the governor or minister of the pigs, the "gentleman pig"; and sometimes say, between jest and earnest, that pigs and bears are good Buddhists. That is because they are not murderous, though strong. It is only in self-defence that they ever do hurt. They live in general without taking life; and a nice she-bear that was sleek and tame was a treat to see, especially as she was not proud, the unpardonable sin in Mongolian eyes. She was ever willing to accept little tit-bits of fruit and to stand and be caressed by anybody.

The woods were near. No doubt she often lifted up her eyes in that direction; but the sweet things of the table and the excitements of the bazaar—all the comforts of Charing Cross, so to speak—kept her from trying to escape.

I once knew a pet that did run away, and after some days' absence came back again; but in this instance, the bear did not worry her master in that way. Servants are not partial to pets. She could go wherever she liked, and perhaps they would not have been sorry if she had departed altogether. But she always came back. Perhaps it was because she could escape at any time, as easily to-morrow as to-day. There was no hurry. She may have intended to go off to the woods at some time or other, and always postponed it. As Goethe admirably says, "We love to walk along the plains, with the summit in our eye."

Whatever her feelings or thoughts, when she took her walks abroad, that is to say, outside her master's little park or compound, she generally went to the bazaar.

7. THE WONDERFUL SUCKLING

ONE of the most amusing of European ways in Burma and India is the habit of adhering to hours of work and fashions of garments that suit London. In the heat of the day the whites and their direct employees are supposed to be working hard. This leaves the best hours of the twenty-four for amusement, which is not exactly what was intended. The fashion is set by men who live in the hills. That is the secret.

You cannot really ignore the sun in the Tropics, however; you can only pretend to do it. Go into many a native quarter or bazaar in the middle of the day, as the bear used to do at Kyauktan, and you behold life honestly relaxed. The customers in the bazaar are country cousins from a distance, if there are any customers. The buzz of an occasional sewing-machine is like the drone of bees in summer, harmonious enough in the ears of the bazaar-sellers, many of whom are taking a siesta.

When she wanted fun or fruit or to see the crowd—when she was on business, so to speak—the bear went to the bazaar like other Kyauktan people, in the morning, or perhaps the late afternoon. When she went in the middle of the day, it was just because master was busy at court and it was dull at home, and a rest seemed likely to be more enjoyable in company.

When once she was sauntering towards it at this mid-day hour, she passed an Indian cottage, in front of which, upon a "charpoy" or bedstead, used also as a couch, and now set upon the ground in a shady spot, a young Indian mother lay sound asleep, with baby in her lap, it may be guessed. At any rate the baby had had enough for the time, while mamma lay back upon the couch, breathing peacefully. Her plump and healthy breasts were full of milk; and as the little bearess looked, the instinct of childhood returned upon her, and she went up softly and laid her lips to the nipple which the other baby had abandoned. "She milked the woman dry," said people afterwards; but nobody saw it being done. Nobody noticed anything till the street rang with female shrieks. "Ayāh! Ayāh! Ayāh! Mother! mother! Help, help! Come, all! Come, all! Come! Come! Come, all! Come, all! Help! help! Ah, mother, mother, mother, mother! Ayāh! Ayāh!" The bear pushed her way through the gathering crowd and hurried home unhurt. One does not readily lift a hand against an old favourite; and she was home before people realised the terrible event.

Luckily for everybody, Kyauktan was, and still is, blessed with that most useful of men—an honest lawyer. He was a barrister-at-law; but the queer convention of some parts of Europe, which restricts the best lawyers to talking in court, and allows them to be consulted only through another lawyer, is as unknown in Burma as in America. At Kyauktan, as in Boston, you do *not* need to be "lathered in one shop and shaved in another." You choose your lawyer, and go to him, straight.

The Kyauktan barrister had been an official once; but, as people said, he had retired and reformed. In sober truth, he had been one of the best Commissioners ever known in Burma; and now his mere presence at Kyauktan made life more bearable to honest men, for many miles around.

To him the husband of the unhappy young mother, just milked dry, went running, a score of women probably shrieking instructions after him, and half the women in Kyauktan standing ready to advise. But, wonderful to tell, there were many of them on the side of the bear, poor harmless orphan; and when, after a while, the obedient husband slowly returned to his wife, and did not announce a suit or anything else to be done, some praised the lawyer, and others said that the man had only pretended to go and consult him. The strangest thing of all, significant of much, was that nobody then complained to the bear's master or even told him of the matter. He was left to learn it later from the bantering of the honest lawyer. Was there ever a pet so popular before?

8. HARUM-SCARUM

THERE were many other freaks of the bear which a kind conspiracy of silence concealed from her master as long as possible. Like other bachelors who live alone, he was not always punctual in sitting down to table. His pet had the healthy appetite of youth, and was hungry at times before dinner was ready, and then, being at home everywhere and not troubled with false pride, she naturally went to the kitchen and helped herself.

It is likely that she burned or scalded herself in that way, for it is known that another little Burman bear, who frequented the kitchen, had that experience. But we have only probability to go upon in this instance. She made no complaints, and returned regularly, and the cook would not tell tales. Indeed, he seems to have taken great pains to protect her, thrusting himself between her and danger so often that, at last, not knowing what he would be at, she either misunderstood his intentions or lost patience, and recollecting how strong she was, she turned to claw that affectionate but too meddlesome cook.

The upshot was all her master was allowed to know. It could not be concealed. The cook had to bolt. Alone in the kitchen, with unfettered discretion, she behaved like the reasonable, civilised animal she was. She merely took what she wanted and did what she liked, and allowed the cook to return. She had never meant to hurt him, only to remove him out of her way.

She used to travel about with her master, when he went on tour. Being unable to ride a pony, she sat in a cart. The ideal method would have been for her to sit in a box or basket on such occasions, and journey as Gulliver did in Brobdingnag; but it was useless to argue with her. She could burst any wickerwork, as easily as Samson burst his bonds, and she saw no need for anything but a convenient seat. She liked to joke with the driver, like a passenger on an old-fashioned bus or coach; but gradually it came to her master's knowledge that, only too often, the driver and anybody else in the cart had to jump down to avoid her—she was so rough in her horseplay. There was a rumour that she once knocked down a driver; but he made no complaint and it was probably an accident. I was once nearly knocked down by a bear that cannoned against me by inadvertence, hurrying to greet me in a friendly way.

When left alone in the cart, she never attempted to touch the reins. She gazed at them and the bullocks, serenely unconcerned, as the passengers in a steamer look at the machinery. When the driver went to the bullocks' heads and stopped them, and gathered up the reins and climbed back into the cart, she seemed to consider his behaviour a matter of course, and looked as if anything else would have surprised her. Nevertheless, when these transporting adventures became known, her master insisted on leaving her at home.

9. ALL THE REST

IT was not altogether disagreeable to the bear to be left alone in the house, with only a servant or two, and nobody to correct her; but she made herself unpleasant to other people. Her master found her, after every absence, "more and more savage" upon his return. These are his own words; and yet, and yet, however imperious to others or contemptuous of humanity, she was always amenable to him, and to him she was always dear.

At this point, as is common in biographies, the historian who would be faithful must face a divided duty. In order to please the friends and relatives, one has to heed nothing but what they choose to tell; and if one does that, then the biography is merely an unreadable fiction. As a satirist cynically puts it, —

> Facts inane the volume fill,
> Keep the secret secret still;
> Here and there may truth be guessed
> From what can be seen—suppressed!

One of the things that make this biography worth writing is the freedom from conventional restraints. So readers shall have the truth, and the whole truth, and nothing but the truth. The bear's master has long been a friend of mine, and I hope will so continue, but truth is dearer than anybody. So I will not suppress the remarks of the honest lawyer at Kyauktan, who is also an old friend, and has read the first draft of this work. He sent me a letter on the subject, containing the excruciating words that the bear at Kyauktan had become "a nuisance." The expression is his. My responsibility is limited to quoting it. I desire to express no opinion of my own.

What her own master could not help seeing was the contrast between her behaviour and that of a very respectable bear at Syriam, a place at the other end of the ridge, nearly a day's walk from Kyauktan, just across the river from Rangoon. The bear living there belonged to Mr Brand of the Burma Oil Company, and he and our heroine's master often compared notes, and discussed the problem of her higher education. Mr Brand seemed to think she had good natural gifts, but had come to a difficult age when she needed *daily* supervision. He never went on tour himself, and was willing to take charge of her. She would be sure to benefit by the company of an older and well-behaved bear, and the two together would be happier at Syriam than either was alone. At last her owner was persuaded, and, when every preliminary had been settled, our heroine set out for her new home (A.D. 1900).

She went in a slow cart, and the day was hot. It is not so well known as it should be that bears and elephants and tigers, too, are almost as sensitive to the sunshine as white men. In this instance, though every possible precaution was taken, the bear was decidedly unhappy on the way. We have to remember that she was an adolescent female and a fully emancipated one, who had lived exclusively for her own amusement, and never had anything particular to do or to suffer in this world. Her sensations, therefore, must have been remarkably like those of the American family, immortalised in Ruskin's letter to Norton of 1869.

"I ... was fated to come from Venice to Verona with an American family, father and mother and two girls—presumably rich—girls 15 and 18. I never before conceived the misery of wretches who had spent all their lives in trying to gratify themselves. It was a little warm—warmer than was entirely luxurious—but nothing in the least harmful. They moaned and fidgeted and frowned and puffed and stretched and fanned, and ate lemons, and smelt bottles, and covered their faces, and tore the cover off again, and had no one thought or feeling, during five hours of travelling in the most noble part of all the world, except what four poor beasts would have had in their den in a menagerie, being dragged about on a hot day...." (*Letters of John Ruskin to C. E. Norton*, I, pp. 218 and 219.)

The longest road has an end, and Syriam was reached at last. The cart stopped, and the bear came down from it with every sensation smothered in one irresistible craving for coolness "Anything to be cool!" A pleasant-looking tank of water was near, and into it she plunged.

The details of what followed are variously reported. Eyes she had and ears of the best; but she used them to avoid people. It was only after a long time that it pleased her to emerge, quite shivering now, cool enough at last.

Fever came on and pneumonia; and, next day she died, and that is the end of the story. When you think of it, that is how every story would end if it went on long enough.

10. HER EPITAPH

IT is now 1910: and already Mr Brand himself is dead; and, spinning in the official whirligig, "like the wind's blast, never resting, homeless," the bear's old master has long ago left Kyauktan, and been in many places. So it is natural that no monument has been put up to her memory; and, maybe, none ever will be. But the things of the spirit are so wonderfully made that words on paper may endure longer than marble or brass; wherefore, though it has not been engraved, let her epitaph be printed. If it is remembered till there is another as long and equally free from falsehood, it may endure for centuries; and, in the far forward dark abysms of time, this little bear may be associated with the constellation of that name, the constellation containing the Polar star. Far stranger things have happened in this wonderful world.

HER EPITAPH

"Here sleeps a bear emancipated,
Who died here young, and died unmated,
Because obedience was not taught her,
And so she stayed too long in water,
When once she wanted to be cool,
And did not know she was a fool:
Her every wish she gratified,
And so she had a chill, and died.

In vain are others' love and care;
The others can't be everywhere.
For sins no neighbours can atone;
We suffer, and we die, alone.
For fine sleek hair and sparkling eyes
Are useless, if you aren't wise;
And things outside you have their laws,
Far stronger than the strongest paws.

So sister-mortals, learn from me!
Take warning if you'd happy be,
To hate the darkness, love the light,
And don't do nothing but what's right;
And listen sometimes now and then,
To what is yelled at you by men;
And so enjoy your lives, instead
Of being, prematurely, dead."

XXXII

A CHINESE HUNTER (740 B.C.)

A STRANGE and vivid glimpse by firelight into distant darkness is given by two Chinese songs, Odes i, vii, 3 and 4, in Legge's *Chinese Classics*, IV, pp. 127 to 131. I have versified Mr Legge's prose. The date was certainly more than 500, and probably 740 B.C., and the locality northern China, probably Honan. Shuh means "younger brother," so that, except to those who believe the commentators, which I cannot, the hero, like the poet, is anonymous,—"*The* younger brother."

Both translations may be sung to the same air, "Scots Wha Ha'e," which was a traditional hunting tune in the south of Scotland.

N.B.—"Ribbons" for reins is a literal translation. That familiar metaphor is over 2600 years old.

I. SHUH HAS OUT A-HUNTING GONE

Shuh has out a-hunting gone;
Men enough are still in town;
But it seems to me there's none,
While I look for you!
People feast and people drive;
Streets are thronged with men alive;
But they're blank till Shuh arrive,
None there are like Shuh!

II. SHUH UPON HIS CHARIOT STANDS

I

Shuh upon his chariot stands;
Takes the ribbons in his hands;
Four bay horses feel commands,
Stepping to and fro.
Regular, like dancers high,
Or the wild geese in the sky,
Insides lead, and outsides nigh,
Like their shoulders, go!

II

At the marsh Shuh stands the first;
Bright the fires around it burst.
Out there springs the tiger curst,
Teeth and claws we meet.
So does Shuh; his arms are bare,
Stops the tiger, kills it there;
Lays the bloody carcass fair
At the prince's feet.

III

Try it not again, my Shuh;
Never hurt we'd see on you!
Once like that for life will do,—
Other game is here.
See him give the horses rein;
Stop, and shoot, and off amain;
Shoot, and hit, and shoot again,
While the fire is clear.

IV

How he brings the horses round!
How the game comes to the ground,
When his arrows kill and wound
Wheresoe'er they go.
Still they go; but, now, they're few;
Now, the quiver's empty too.
Home! The steeds the stable view,
Yet they're coming slow!

In the classical texts, these ancient hunting-songs appear as here translated; but in singing them, if there is time to spare, the first may well be sung *after* the second as well as before it. It is at once a fit introduction and a fit conclusion.

These two songs are taken from a collection of *Chinese Songs and Sayings*, not published yet, and put here to show a kind of tiger-killing deserving as much honour as men can ever give a fellow-man.

In those days hunting was more like work than sport, and tigers were still a menace to humanity, such as we can hardly now conceive. There was great merit in hindering a tiger from escaping then; but to-day that matters little. Such an event as the song describes is not uncommon still. I have heard credibly of about a dozen like it among contemporaries in Burma in the last twenty-four years. Men seeking deer or other game are suddenly confronted by a tiger similarly engaged. If the men make way for him, he merely shows his teeth and swiftly escapes, and that is what generally happens. But if any one of the hunters hurts him, or his road seems blocked, then there is danger; and that is how fatal accidents often happen.

Something of that sort was probably impending on this occasion, 740 B.C., or about then. There was probably a big crowd and a desperate tiger, and while the others facing him were shrinking, Shuh perhaps leaped from his chariot, certainly stepped to the front, ready for action, a stalwart Chinese figure, stripped to the waist, like Nelson's sailors on a day of battle, and in all likelihood a big-pointed knife in his hand. A shout might make the tiger shy a second, and so give him a chance; but the likeliest thing is that the tiger, coming out of the darkness into the glare of the fires, did not see him, and perhaps was trying to get away, or charging some other person, so that Shuh could take him sideways and kill him. Somehow or other, Shuh did it. Think of the few thrilling seconds of glorious life, and the jubilation of the crowd when the knife went home.

Note the difference between them and us. Miss your shot with the breechloader, and you can fire again, and even if you do not hit a vital part, you can stop him. "But with bow and arrows," as an old man said to me in 1889, telling how he and his father had fought a tiger with such weapons, and showing me the good old cross-bow they used, "it is folly to shoot till he is close, for at a distance the arrow merely irritates him. Wait till he is near."

"Ten yards?"

"My father, let him come nearer. Then you hit his brain through the eye, if he's coming straight, or the heart through the ribs, if he shows his side, and so he is dead."

"But if he isn't dead?"

"Then drop your bow, and fight him with the knife. Never try a second shot, for, if you do, he's sure to get you. The tiger is very, *very* quick. You have to dodge him and get a knife into his vitals before he grips you."

I suggested a spear; but was told it was too clumsy and slow to be a good weapon.

The words of that old veteran, living among the hills between Burma and China, seemed to me to illuminate the hunting scene in old Honan better than any of the commentators on the Classics. But for his talk, one would have been slow to guess that Shuh went close to the tiger with a knife. That would explain why the poet alluded to Shuh's bare arms, and to his standing in the front. He could not have fired arrows from his chariot, for the horses would have bolted. So we may still see him through so many centuries, afoot and in front, with business-like bare arms and sharp knife ready; we can rejoice with them all, and admire him yet, and feel also, with the singers, "once like that for life will do." It comes like a shock to remember that we are among the shades, and that more than fifty or sixty generations of men have come and gone since Shuh and his companions all melted into dust and air.

It gives us another kind of shock to contrast that kind of work with modern hunting. Our statesmen at large, slaughtering in foreign woods, are neither better nor worse than their friends at home, "the poulterers." The only serious danger is from their own awkwardness in handling guns. Their butcheries are like those in old Roman arenas; and even Theodore Roosevelt himself, returning in gory glory but without a scratch from Africa, can only be compared by one of his admirers to the immortal Tartarin of Tarascon.

Lector House believes that a society develops through a two-fold approach of continuous learning and adaptation, which is derived from the study of classic literary works spread across the historic timeline of literature records. Therefore, we aim at reviving, repairing and redeveloping all those inaccessible or damaged but historically as well as culturally important literature across subjects so that the future generations may have an opportunity to study and learn from past works to embark upon a journey of creating a better future.

This book is a result of an effort made by Lector House towards making a contribution to the preservation and repair of original ancient works which might hold historical significance to the approach of continuous learning across subjects.

HAPPY READING & LEARNING!

LECTOR HOUSE LLP
E-MAIL: lectorpublishing@gmail.com